Colonialism

Short Histories of Big Ideas Series List

Colonialism

NORRIE MACQUEEN

Harlow, England • London • New York • Boston • San Francisco • Toronto
Sydney • Tokyo • Singapore • Hong Kong • Seoul • Taipei • New Delhi
Cape Town • Madrid • Mexico City • Amsterdam • Munich • Paris • Milan

PEARSON EDUCATION LIMITED

Edinburgh Gate
Harlow CM20 2JE
United Kingdom
Tel: +44 (0)1279 623623
Fax: +44 (0)1279 431059
Website: www.pearsoned.co.uk

First edition published in Great Britain in 2007

ISBN: 978-1-4058-4630-1

British Library Cataloguing in Publication Data
A catalogue record for this book can be obtained from the British Library

10 9 8 7 6 5 4 3 2 1
11 10 09 08 07

Set in IowanOldSt BT 9/15pt by 3
Printed in Malaysia (CTP-VVP)

The Publisher's policy is to use paper manufactured from sustainable forests.

For Alice and Sophie, Jack and Jamie

Because colonization is the extension of the mother country, the history which the colonist writes is not that of the despoiled country, but the history of his own nation.

Frantz Fanon

Contents

Series Editor's Preface

WHAT MAKES THE WORLD MOVE? Great men? Irresistible forces? Catastrophic events?

When listening to the morning news on the radio, reading our daily newspapers, following debates on the internet, watching evening television, all of these possibilities – and more – are offered as explanations of the troubles that beset the world in the Middle East, the 'war on terror' in Iraq and Afghanistan, environmental disasters at Chernobyl or New Orleans, and genocide in Sudan or Rwanda.

Where should we look to find answers to the puzzles of the present? To psychology? To economics? To sociology? To political science? To philosophy? Each of these disciplines offers insights into the personalities and the subterranean forces that propel the events that change the world, and within each of these disciplines there are experts who dissect current affairs on the foundation of these insights.

But all of these events, these problems, and even these disciplines themselves have one thing in common: they have a history. And it is through an understanding of the history of those ideas that inspired the people behind the events, and the ideas behind the ideologies that attempted to explain and control the forces around them that we can comprehend the perplexing and confusing world of the present day.

'Short Histories of Big Ideas' aims to provide readers with clear, concise and readable explanations of those ideas that were instrumental in shaping the twentieth century and that continue to shape – and reshape – the present. Everyone who attempts to follow the events of today via the newspapers, television, radio and the internet cannot help but see or hear references to 'capitalism', 'communism', 'feminism', 'environmentalism', 'nationalism', 'colonialism' and many other 'isms'. And, while most of us probably believe that we have a basic understanding of what these terms mean, we are probably much less certain about who it was that coined, invented or defined them. Even more murky is our understanding of how these concepts moved from an idea to become an ideology and, perhaps, a phenomenon that changed the world. Most bewildering may be the disputes and controversies between factions and divisions within the movements and political parties that claim to be the true followers and the legitimate heirs of those who first conceived of the concepts to which they claim to adhere.

The authors of these Short Histories have been asked to write accessible, jargon-free prose with the goal of making comprehensible to the intelligent, interested but non-expert reader these highly complicated concepts. In each instance the approach taken is chronological, as each author attempts to explain the origins of these ideas, to describe the people who created them and then to follow the twisting path they followed from conception to the present. Each author in the series is an expert in the field, with a mastery of the literature on the subject – and a desire to convey to readers the knowledge and the understanding that the research of specialist scholars has produced, but which is normally inaccessible to those not engaged in studying these subjects in an academic environment.

The work of specialists often seems remote, obscure, even pedantic, to the non-specialist, but the authors in this series are committed to the goal of bringing the insights and understanding of specialists to a wider public, to concerned citizens and general readers who wish to go beyond today's headlines and form a more comprehensive and meaningful picture of today's world.

Gordon Martel

Preface

THIS IS A BOOK ABOUT COLONIALISM, perhaps the single most powerful force shaping the world we inhabit. There are very few aspects of either high politics or daily life in the twenty-first century not affected to some degree by the colonial experience of the past hundred and fifty years. The apparently endless conflicts in Africa, the cauldron of the Middle East, the dangerous frontiers of south Asia – these are all in some ways legacies of Europe's irruption into other continents during that time. The inheritance has been widely spread. The fabric of contemporary life in both the South and the North of the globe is woven from the threads of colonialism. At the beginning of the twenty-first century social manners, popular culture, eating habits, dress – and ultimately the world's gene-pool – have all been altered and conditioned by the colonial experience.

Major dramas in the politics of west European countries have been scripted by colonialism. The Spanish Civil War began in 1936 in the garrisons of North Africa. France was dragged to the edge of the abyss in 1958 by its disastrous war in Algeria. In 1974 the Portuguese revolution was provoked by the hopelessness of the country's situation in Africa. Elsewhere, in Britain for example, the effect has been less spectacular but still immensely important in national life.

At an individual level we Europeans are often unaware of – or perhaps simply take for granted – the extent to which colonialism has shaped our own life histories. A personal audit can be very revealing. In my own case, I was born in Glasgow at a time when it was still proud to call itself 'the second city of the empire'. Now it is usually described as a 'post-industrial' city, but it would be as accurately called 'post-colonial'. An Atlantic port, it was a city born from the wealth of the plantation colonies of the Americas. This history is still evident in its central thoroughfares: Tobago Street, Virginia Street, St Vincent Place, Jamaica Bridge. By some accounts it is to be seen too in the notorious sugar addiction that has long afflicted the eating habits of west-central Scotland. My father spent his working life in a factory which made machinery for the Caribbean sugar plantations. My uncles had worked in the shipyards which were still, in the mid-twentieth century, essential to the network of imperial trade and population movement. The religious education of the time and place, at least that provided by Church of Scotland Sunday Schools, seemed to be preoccupied by the life, work and example of David Livingstone in the Dark Continent. We were perhaps the last generation of children to routinely collect stamps and we disdained the odd shapes and lurid colours of European philately in favour of the sepia sobriety of the empire issues. These transported us to previously unheard of specks on the map: St Lucia, the New Hebrides, Tristan da Cunha, the Gilbert and Ellis Islands. They were places, however distant and exotic, somehow made safe and familiar by having stamps with values in shillings and pence and the head of the monarch in the corner. Later, such innocent imperial sentiment was abandoned in embarrassment amidst the atmosphere of anti-colonial radicalism that infused western Europe in the 1970s. Then, it seemed to me to be perfectly natural to go to Mozambique to 'work for the revolution' in the grim aftermath of its sudden decolonization. A few years later the same sense of a special relationship with the post-colonial world took me for several years to Papua New Guinea. Today the nationalities of my research students – Nigerian, Bangladeshi, Ghanaian – reflect another dimension to the enduring relationships forged by colonialism. The details and emphasis will vary, but the degree to which the colonial phenomenon has shaped my own life is not as untypical for Britons of my age and background as might be imagined.

This book aims to offer an overview, though necessarily a brief one, of the forces that so moulded the worlds of both colonized and colonizer. Yet, as the brief autobiography I have just presented indicates, it is a book written by a 'colonizer' (however reluctant I may be to acknowledge the fact). As such, its European focus is sharper than its colonial one. I make no apology for this. We are all products of our place and time and this unavoidably shapes our world views. The lines from Frantz Fanon which are used as an epigraph for this book were chosen to convey this at the outset. The history of the former colonial world should properly be written by the people of that world.

Colonialism is obviously not unique to the modern age, nor is it an inherently European activity. Colonial power has been exercised in some form throughout recorded human history and in all corners of the globe. It was pursued by imperial entities from China to West Africa and from Persia to Rome. Nor, arguably, is colonialism necessarily either a 'formal' or an 'international' activity. Informal – or 'semi' – colonialism – was imposed by

Europe on nominally independent countries like Thailand and Ethiopia while their neighbours in south-east Asia and sub-Saharan Africa were subjected to the formal variety. Similarly, 'internal colonialism', the exploitation of a country's geographical and ethnic periphery by its dominant centre, has been identified across the world from the British Isles to the United States. However, in this book the focus is on the overseas colonialism of Europe of the past century and a half.

General orientations are needed, though. The so-called 'new imperialism' of the nineteenth and twentieth centuries did not appear in a historical vacuum, and if it is to be properly understood its genealogy should be traced. The 'other end' of the colonial experience is immensely important too. The imperial aftermath is its enduring legacy to the contemporary world. This inheritance is controversial, to say the least. Fierce debates continue about the nature of 'neo-colonialism' and 'post-colonialism'. Therefore, while the primary focus of the book is the colonial interlude itself, the 'before' and the 'after' will be explored as well.

The core of this vast historical process, the most intense period of European colonialism, is to be found in the last two decades of the nineteenth century and the first of the twentieth. In these few years a small number of European powers controlled the greater part of the surface of the planet. It was an episode with consequences which, for good or ill, have set the terms of millions of contemporary lives, as we have said. There is every sign that the twenty-first century will be as profoundly marked by the experience as the twentieth. My hope is that this book, limited in length and range as it is, will identify and illuminate the key vehicles and routes by which this enormous, multilayered influence has been brought to bear on our lives, those of our children and, undoubtedly, on those of our grandchildren as well.

Perth, Scotland
February 2007

Timeline I
Modern colonialism
A chronology

1492	Columbus lands in the Americas
1494	Treaty of Tordesillas
1600	British East India Company formed
1602	Netherlands East India Company formed
1651/1663	British Navigation Acts
1662	Dutch 'purchase' Manhattan Island
1707	British Act of Union (England and Scotland)
1756–63	The 'Seven Years War'
1776	(British) American Independence
1807	Britain declares Atlantic slave trade illegal
1857–8	Indian Mutiny against British rule
1884–5	Berlin Conference on partition of Africa
1890	British ultimatum to Portugal on expansion in central Africa
1896	Defeat of Italy by Abyssinia at Adowa
1898	Fashoda crisis (Anglo-French rivalry)
1898	Spanish-American War

1902   Hobson's *Imperialism* published

1905/1911   Moroccan crises (Franco-German rivalry)

1910   Japan occupies Korean peninsula

1914   Outbreak of the First World War

1916   Lenin's *Imperialism: Highest Stage of Capitalism* pub-
            lished

1917   Bolshevik Revolution in Russia

1919   Versailles Conference and creation of the League
            of Nations

1922   Lugard's *The Dual mandate in Tropical Africa* pub-
            lished

1931   Statute of Westminster – sovereignty of British
            'white dominions' recognized

1935   Italian attack on Abyssinia

1939   Outbreak of Second World War in Europe

1941   Outbreak of Second World War in Asia

1945   End of the Second World War and establishment
            of the United Nations

1948   Britain withdraws from Palestine Mandate; cre-
            ation of the state of Israel

1950–3   Korean War

1952   Frantz Fanon's *Black Skin, White Masks* published

1954   French defeated by Vietnamese nationalist forces
            at Dien Bien Phu

1954   Liberation war begins in Algeria

1956   Suez crisis

1957   Treaty of Rome signed (European Economic
            Community)

1958   Charles de Gaulle becomes president of France
            amidst Algerian crisis

1960	UN General Assembly adopts the 'Declaration on the Granting of Independence to Colonial Countries and Peoples'
	UN peacekeeping operation begins in the Congo
1961	India expels Portugal from Goa
1961	Liberation wars begin in Portuguese Africa
1962–3	UN administration in West New Guinea (Irian Jaya) – transfer of territory to Indonesia
1964	UN operation in Cyprus begins
1965	White rebellion and unilateral declaration of independence in Southern Rhodesia
1967–70	Biafran rebellion and civil war in Nigeria
1973	US military withdrawal from Vietnam
1974	Portuguese revolution (precursor to rapid decolonization in Africa)
1979	Islamic revolution in Iran
1983	US invasion of Grenada
1989	Fall of Berlin Wall
1989–90	UN operation in Namibia
1991	Break-up of the Soviet Union
1993	Eritrea separates from Ethiopia
1994	Majority rule in South Africa
1999	Britain returns Hong Kong to China
2001	Terrorist attacks on the United States – beginning of 'War on Terror'
1999–2002	UN administration of East Timor

Timeline II
European decolonization
since 1940

Country (Contemporary Name)	Year	Colonial Power
Middle East		
Lebanon	1943	France (League Mandate)
Jordan	1946	Britain (League Mandate)
Syria	1946	France (League Mandate)
Israel (Palestine)	1948	Britain (League Mandate)
Kuwait	1961	Britain
South Yemen (Aden)	1967	Britain
Bahrain	1971	Britain
Qatar	1971	Britain
United Arab Emirates	1971	Britain
Asia		
Indonesia	1945	Holland (recognized 1949)
Vietnam	1945	France (recognized 1954)
India	1947	Britain

Pakistan	1947	Britain (Bangladesh secedes 1971)
Burma	1948	Britain
Sri Lanka	1948	Britain
Laos	1949	France
Cambodia	1953	France
Malaysia/Singapore	1957	Britain
Brunei	1984	Britain
East Timor	2002	Portugal via Indonesia

North Africa

Libya	1951	Italy (expelled 1942)
Morocco	1956	France
Tunisia	1956	France
Algeria	1962	France

Sub-Saharan Africa

Sudan	1956	Egypt/Britain
Ghana	1957	Britain
Guinea	1958	France
Benin	1960	France
Burkina Faso	1960	France
Cameroon	1960	France (UN Trusteeship)
Central Africa Republic	1960	France
Chad	1960	France
Congo (DRC)	1960	Belgium
Côte d'Ivoire	1960	France
Gabon	1960	France

Mali	1960	France
Mauritania	1960	France
Niger	1960	France
Nigeria	1960	Britain
Senegal	1960	France
Somalia	1960	Italy (UN Trusteeship)/Britain
Togo	1960	France
Rwanda	1961	Belgium (UN Trusteeship)
Sierra Leone	1961	Britain
Burundi	1962	Belgium (UN Trusteeship)
Uganda	1962	Britain
Kenya	1963	Britain
Tanzania	1964	Britain
Malawi	1964	Britain
Zambia	1964	Britain
Gambia	1965	Britain
Botswana	1966	Britain
Lesotho	1966	Britain
Swaziland	1968	Britain
Equatorial Guinea	1968	Spain
Guinea-Bissau	1974	Portugal
Angola	1975	Portugal
Cape Verde	1975	Portugal
Mozambique	1975	Portugal
S. Tomé e Príncipe	1975	Portugal
Djibouti	1977	France
Zimbabwe	1980	Britain via white rebel regime
Namibia	1990	South Africa (UN Trusteeship)
Eritrea	1993	Italy via Ethiopia

Indian Ocean

Madagascar	1960	France
Maldives	1965	Britain
Mauritius	1968	Britain
Comoros	1975	France
Seychelles	1976	Britain

Caribbean and Latin America

Jamaica	1962	Britain
Trinidad and Tobago	1962	Britain
Barbados	1966	Britain
Guyana	1966	Britain
Bahamas	1973	Britain
Grenada	1974	Britain
Suriname	1975	Holland
Dominica	1978	Britain
St Lucia	1979	Britain
St Vincent/Grenadines	1979	Britain
Belize	1980	Britain
Antigua and Barbuda	1981	Britain
St Kitts and Nevis	1983	Britain

South Pacific

Samoa	1962	New Zealand (UN Trusteeship)
Nauru	1968	Australia (UN Trusteeship)
Fiji	1970	Britain

Tonga	1970	Britain
Papua New Guinea	1975	Australia (UN Trusteeship)
Solomon Islands	1978	Britain
Tuvalu	1978	Britain
Kiribati	1979	Britain
Vanuatu	1980	Britain/France

Europe

| Cyprus | 1960 | Britain |
| Malta | 1964 | Britain |

CHAPTER 1

European colonialism before the 'new imperialism'

COLONIALISM DID NOT BEGIN in the nineteenth century. The 'new imperialism' which began at that time did not spring spontaneously as a fully formed policy from the royal courts and chancelleries of Europe. Logically it could only be 'new' if it replaced something older. In many key respects colonialism grew organically from a long narrative of European imperial expansion in the post-medieval world, one that began with the Spanish and Portuguese empires which were established in the fifteenth century.

Of course, it is possible to push the narrative back further still. No historical phenomenon or phase of international politics ever appears from anything other than a long process. The Iberian colonialism which followed the 'discoveries' of the great navigators of the fifteenth and sixteenth centuries itself looked back to the Mediterranean empires of Genoa and Venice in the fourteenth century. These in turn had roots in the imperialism of the European crusades to the Middle East. The Christian zeal that helped drive those crusades itself began in the eastern colonies of Rome a millennium before. Moving forward, Spanish and Portuguese colonialism did not suddenly mutate into the new imperialism in the nineteenth century. Their empires were just early episodes in a continuous sequence of colonization which led to the European scramble for tropical colonies five centuries later. In the seventeenth century the Netherlands emerged as a major colonial power, displacing Portugal from many of its colonial possessions in Asia (and for a time in Africa as well). By the eighteenth century Britain had become the predominant seaborne imperialist and, despite persistent challenges from France, managed to hold this position up until the mid-nineteenth century on the eve of the 'new' imperialism.

There were other countries involved in the economic exploitation of lands beyond Europe between the sixteenth and nineteenth centuries. Denmark, perhaps an unlikely colonial power in the light of its contemporary international image, had a string of trading colonies in India, West Africa and the Caribbean. Although most of these were sold on to Britain and France in the eighteenth and early nineteenth centuries, the residue of the 'Danish West Indies' disappeared only in 1917 when Denmark's portion of the Virgin Islands passed to the United States. To the east, Russia was pressing into central Asia in the late sixteenth and the seventeenth centuries, laying the foundations of the great Czarist empire which in the nineteenth century would challenge Britain's Indian one in the so-called 'Great Game'. The history of European colonialism, then, is one of overlapping national histories and interconnected geographies rather than one of sudden discontinuities.

Portugal and Spain in Asia and the Americas

However crowded Europe's colonial world was to become, the dominance of Spain and Portugal was more or less total until the end of the six-teenth century. Although physically bound together in the Iberian peninsula and

However crowded Europe's colonial world was to become, the dominance of Spain and Portugal was more or less total until the end of the sixteenth century.

sharing a complex and often violent history, Spain and Portugal managed their respective colonial adventures without too much friction. In large part this was because virtually the entire world was available to them at the outset and, though conflicts did occur, they were managed in a larger context of apparently lim-itless opportunity.

The colonial ventures of both countries were inextricably entwined with maritime exploration. Just as the new imperialism five centuries later would be driven on by European technical advances like steam power and telegraphy, the Iberian *conquistas* were made possible by new navigation aids like the astrolabe and reliable compasses and by the development of the fast, ocean-going *caravella*. Conveniently, the two Iberian powers looked outwards from the edge of Europe in generally different directions. Given their position on the western extreme of the continent both were clearly Atlantic powers. But while Spanish colonial ambitions fol-lowed Christopher Columbus west into the Americas, Portugal was more interested, initially at any rate, in the east. Lisbon commanded the sea-routes to Asia via Africa's Atlantic seaboard already explored by Vasco da Gama and the other fifteenth-century *navigadores*.

These separate territorial interests were formalized in the Treaty of Tordesillas in 1494. Perfectly in tune with the cultural assumptions of the era, this effectively divided 'ownership' of the world beyond Europe between the two countries. The agreement followed a papal bull issued by Pope Alexander VI at the urging of Ferdinand and Isabella of Spain. Quickly realizing the potential wealth to be extracted from the New World in which Columbus had just landed, the Spanish rulers persuaded the (Spanish-born) Pope to declare Spain's exclusive rights to the Americas. However, the original line of demarcation between the segments of the world assigned to Portugal and Spain that ran north to south through the Atlantic not only excluded Portugal from the American continent, as intended, but drastically narrowed its Atlantic routes down Africa to Asia as well. At Tordesillas the line was adjusted westwards to guarantee Portugal's continued freedom of movement off the West African coast. Significantly for the history of Latin America, this had the coincidental effect of shifting the seaboard of what was to become Brazil into Portugal's sector, ensuring that the largest and most populous state of Latin America would emerge from Portuguese rather than Spanish colonialism.

Brazil would come to form the centrepiece of Portugal's so-called Second Empire in the later seventeenth and eighteenth century, but only after the decline of the First Empire which was firmly located in Asia (the Third and last Portuguese Empire was in Africa in the nineteenth and twentieth centuries). Although Portuguese colonization had begun with the occupation of Madeira, the Azores and parts of North Africa early in the fifteenth century, Asia was seen to offer the greatest economic returns in the form of spices, precious metals and oriental manufactures and Portugal remained the dominant European power in Asia throughout the sixteenth century. It presided over a trading empire stretching from the Middle East to modern-day Malaysia, Indonesia, India and Japan. With the lease of Macau in 1557 (relinquished only in 1999) Portuguese traders also gained access to the vast riches of China.

The Portuguese possessions that comprised this First Empire were essentially trading posts. They were certainly not 'colonies of settlement'. Portugal's human presence was transitory for the most part. Nor were these territories true 'colonies of exploit-ation'; they merely provided doors to trade with larger hinterlands that Portugal saw no advantage in attempting to col-onize. Such a task would probably have been beyond its capacities anyway. From their coastal strongholds the Portuguese would usually enlist the services of local agents who could smooth the process of trade and ensure that its terms favoured their employers. These were called *compradores* (literally 'buyers'), a term that would find a new significance in the debates over 'neo-colonialism' in the late twentieth century.

Spain in the meantime was consolidating and extending its presence in the Americas. Here its primary modus operandi was violent conquest rather than commercial penetration as pursued by the Portuguese in Asia. Spanish colonization moved outwards from the initial landing points of Columbus in the Caribbean. In the first half of the fifteenth century Cuba and the island of Hispaniola (today composed of Haiti and the Dominican Republic) were colonized. Attention then shifted to the adjacent part of the continental landmass with the conquest of Panama and Mexico. From Central America the mythic riches of the southern part of the continent beckoned. The major cultural consequence of this Spanish avarice was the destruction of long-established and hitherto stable indigenous societies among which the Aztecs of Mexico and the Incas of Peru are the best known.

The driving belief in the myth of an 'eldorado', a land of gold, which powered Spain's expansion throughout Central and South America, said much about the nature of Spanish colonialism.

The driving belief in the myth of an 'eldorado', a land of gold, which powered Spain's expansion throughout Central and South America, said much about the nature of Spanish colonialism. The first priority was bullion which could simply be transported back to Spain (the name 'Argentina', for example, means literally the 'place of silver'). The inflow of gold and silver, particularly to Castile, Spain's dominant component kingdom, was immense, particularly during the 'Golden Age' of Philip II, who ruled between 1556 and 1598. This rush of wealth from 'New Spain', as the American colonies were called, had a distorting effect on the development of the Spanish economy during the sixteenth century. It fuelled a false prosperity amidst which local industry and commerce failed to flourish. With an apparently infinite supply of precious metals on tap, why develop local manufacturing when all requirements, whether necessities or luxuries, could be bought as imports?

Ironically, this mindset was also common in post-colonial states in the twentieth century. Countries like Zambia in southern Africa and Nauru in the Pacific chose to rely on the sale of natural resources first exploited by their colonial occupiers (copper and phosphates respectively). This was seen as a viable route to prosperity and 'modernity', in preference to the harder but more sustainable road of agricultural and industrial development. In sixteenth-century New Spain, as in the twentieth-century Third World, the results were deeply damaging. When the tap was turned off – as it inevitably was in both settings – through natural depletion and uncertain world prices, all that remained were underdeveloped economies unable to operate effectively in a competitive international environment. The seventeenth century thus saw Spain's colonial vanities exposed. Persistent war between shifting European alliances revealed the fundamental weakness of metropolitan Spain lying below the gilded splendour of the colonial empire. Spanish control of its vast American territories began to unravel. Repeatedly bested in conflict with England and France, Spain experienced a fall in its relative standing in Europe. Spain's decline at this time in fact shaped the future of the European colonialism. When, at the beginning of the seventeenth century, it lost its continental colonies in the Netherlands, the circumstances were put in place for the rise of a new powerful Dutch colonial empire.

One consequence of the Spanish policy of plunder – and the ethnocide that went with it – was that, after the moveable wealth of Latin America had been seized and sent back to Europe, Spain was left in possession of huge areas which could be turned into colonies of settlement. The weakness of the European metropolitan centre meant that the migrant communities which developed in these American territories were largely left to themselves. The political consequence of this was that by the eighteenth century a de facto autonomy had been established in the nominally Spanish colonies throughout the American continent. The northernmost of these came under pressure first from France and then from a new actor, the emergent United States. Louisiana and Florida slipped from Spanish control. Then, in the first decades of the nineteenth century, new republics were declared throughout South and Central America, a process that an increasingly enfeebled Spain was unable to resist.

In the meantime, Portugal's altogether less dramatic colonial presence in Asia had also declined. Here the problem was not settler rebellion but displacement by a new and vigorous colonial competitor: Holland. The process of decline of the two Iberian empires was linked. Between the 1580s and 1640s Portugal had been ruled by the Spanish monarchy. In the earlier part of this period, during the powerful reign of Philip II, Portugal's colonial empire benefited from the arrangement, particularly from the support of Spain's naval strength. But as Spain declined in the latter stages of the union, Portugal suffered in its wake. One of the key events in this was the independence, unification and subsequent florescence of the Netherlands. The new Dutch seaborne empire which emerged after the expulsion of Spain from the Low Countries was to be Portugal's nemesis in Asia.

Only a few fragments of Portugal's First Empire in Asia remained in the twentieth century when their odd circumstances turned them into international causes célèbres.

Only a few fragments of Portugal's First Empire in Asia remained in the twentieth century when their odd circumstances turned them into international causes célèbres. In 1961 the Indian army expelled the Portuguese from the enclave of Goa in the west of the subcontinent. While the Portuguese dictatorship of the time reacted with outrage, the rest of the world responded with studied indifference. Further east and south, Portugal retained the eastern part of the island of Timor in the Indonesian archipelago, which it had held surrounded by the Dutch East Indies and then independent Indonesia. In 1975, however, revolution in Portugal had raised the possibility of an independent East Timor under a Marxist regime. The Indonesian military regime invaded the territory with tacit western support and imposed a bloody repression which lasted for the next quarter-century. East Timor eventually became an independent state in 2002 under United Nations sponsorship following a violent separation from Indonesia.

These were peculiarities, however, exceptions to the larger disintegration in the seventeenth century. The effect of the loss of the Asian empire was to shift Lisbon's imperial attention to the Second Empire in Brazil. Here once again the fortunes of the two Iberian colonial empires merged. Brazil declared its own independence amidst the more general collapse of Spanish rule in the continent-wide convulsion of settler-led nationalism in the first decades of the nineteenth century.

The Dutch in Asia and beyond

With the decline of Spanish sea-power (hastened by the failure of the Armada against England in 1588), the Netherlands became the dominant European maritime nation and remained so for much of the following century. The Dutch approach to colonial expansion – which in the seventeenth century was a concomitant part of this naval power – was closer to the

Portuguese trading model than the Spanish expansionist one. Perhaps inevitably, therefore, it was Portugal that became the main victim of the rise of the Netherlands as the Dutch displaced it from its trading colonies in Asia.

Reflecting the commercial character of Dutch colonialism, the key agent of expansion was a trading venture, the United East India Company, which was established by the Netherlands government in 1602. With its base in the port of Batavia in Java (now Jakarta, the capital of Indonesia), the Company lay at the hub of a relentlessly expanding network of trading colonies. The Portuguese were ejected from their Asian possessions one by one. First, Holland's naval power, projected from Java, allowed its traders and administrators to oust their Portuguese counterparts throughout the Indonesian archipelago (with the exception of East Timor). Then, by the middle of the seventeenth century, the Portuguese had been forced out of Ceylon (Sri Lanka) and Malacca (in modern-day Malaysia). Only in its trade with China did Portugal manage to keep ahead of the Dutch, largely because of its privileged position in Macau (though even here the Dutch attempted to move in on their rivals by establishing themselves for a time in Formosa – modern-day Taiwan – off the south China coast).

In truth, it was not just the superior sea-power of the Netherlands that helped the Dutch push Portugal from most of Asia. The economics of Portuguese colonialism had always been more complex than the simple plunder-based approach of Spain. Trade is by definition a two-way process and the oriental produce brought back to Europe had to be paid for, even if the terms of exchange were favourable to Portugal. Having little in the way of manufactures to trade, Portuguese merchants paid with gold and silver. The profits from the on-sale of Asian products beyond Portugal eventually failed to balance the depletion of the national treasury. The situation was worsened by the political and economic geography of seventeenth-century Europe. Lisbon, on the western edge of the continent, was not the best base for the onward trading of Asian imports. To reach the prosperous markets of northern Europe, spices and other produce had to be sent on further long, expensive and often hazardous journeys. In contrast, the Netherlands ports, as well as serving the newly prosperous Holland itself, were close to the best markets in France and England. In these parts of Europe the habits and lifestyle of entire populations were changing irreversibly as a result of the new luxuries – tea, coffee and tobacco as well as spices – arriving from overseas. In the meantime Portuguese society failed to develop in the face of the linked decline of the national economy and national self-confidence.

Although Asia was the major focus of Holland's colonial interest in the seventeenth century, its empire was truly global. Like the Portuguese, the Dutch had

Although Asia was the major focus of Holland's colonial interest in the seventeenth century, its empire was truly global.

established fortified possessions in Africa. These were not primary colonies but essential way-stations on the sea-route to Asia. Cape Town was founded in the middle of the century and, unusually in the Dutch colonial project, it eventually grew to form the base for an extensive colony of settlement. The Dutch who first migrated to southern Africa at this time were the ancestors of the Boers who fought the British in the nineteenth century and of the Afrikaners who ruled Apartheid South Africa until the end of the twentieth century. The Portuguese found themselves on the receiving end of Dutch ambitions in Africa as well. On the western seaboard they were forced out of their fortified ports on the coast of Angola for a time, though they were able to re-establish themselves after a few years, in what would become the jewel of the Third (African) Portuguese Empire.

The Netherlands also had a major colonial interest in the Americas, both north and south, in the seventeenth century. A Dutch West Indies company was established to perform the same state-supervised trading functions as its counterpart in Asia. The Portuguese were the victims here too when the Dutch attempted to take over parts of the coast of Brazil. More enduring colonies were established further north in Guyana and Suriname (which became independent only in 1975). In the Caribbean the British Virgin Islands were previously a Dutch possession (just as those of the United States had been Danish). The greatest Dutch impact in the Americas was made further north, however. In 1626 Manhattan Island was 'bought' from the native inhabitants for sixty Dutch guilders. New Amsterdam, as it was then called, had a short-lived but busy existence as a Dutch colony of settlement until it was seized by the English in the 1660s prior to being re-christened New York.

Eventually, Dutch colonial power, like that of Portugal in Asia, waned as comparative advantage shifted. The power of nations in seventeenth-century Europe, an era of more or less constant warfare within and between states, was highly fluid. Whatever the extent of its seaborne empire, Holland, like Portugal, was a relatively small country within an inherently unstable European system of states. In this uncertain environment the achievements of the Netherlands, judged in terms of colonial power, were remarkable for a country of its size, population and strategically precarious location. The twentieth-century consequences of Dutch colonialism – from south-east Asia to southern Africa – were comparable in their significance to those of the much larger imperial nations.

France in North America and India

The colonial adventures of Holland's large and powerful neighbour, France, were patchy in the seventeenth and eighteenth centuries. Local preoccupations, within France and between it and its west European rivals, constrained colonial projects in distant parts of the world.

French interest in the Americas lay mainly in Canada, which had the potential to rival Britain's colonies of settlement further south in New England, Virginia and the Carolinas. Fur trading posts were established in the first years of the seventeenth century in Nova Scotia and then, more substantially, at Quebec. The relationship between the Francophone and Anglophone parts of Canada which grew from this early colonial phase remained difficult into the twentieth century, at times violently so. Beyond New France, as French Canada became known, the French also had a presence in the Caribbean where Britain was becoming a major actor in the seventeenth century. Guadeloupe and Martinique were colonized by France. So was Haiti, where France took possession of the first European landing points in the Americas from Spain. These islands were plantation colonies, providing France with sugar and other tropical produce. In the 1660s France also established the colony of

Guiana on the mainland of South America (where the notorious Devil's Island penal colony was later located). Martinique, Guadeloupe and Guiana were never decolonized and remain *départements* of metropolitan France to this day. French explorers also opened the way for their king's colonization of parts of North America in the lower Mississippi region. The French colonial interlude here, though relatively short, has left its mark on place names in the southern United States. The state of Louisiana, its main city New Orleans and its state capital Baton Rouge are obvious examples.

By the late seventeenth century French interest also fell on India. Here, as in the Americas, France came into conflict with English (later British) interests, having first tangled with the Dutch. Extravagant French plans for south Asia came to little in the face of this competition. A French East India Company was formed to rival those of the Dutch and the British but it achieved nothing like their commercial success. The cost of the long conflict with Britain at the beginning of the eighteenth century, as well as restive local populations, made the Indian venture fundamentally uneconomic for France. Nevertheless, small French enclaves remained (as with Portuguese Goa) within India even after its independence from Britain in 1947. The largest of these, Pondicherry in the south-east, was given up in the 1950s, by which time France was preoccupied with the dramas surrounding the last days of a later – and at least for a time more successful – phase of colonization in North Africa and south-east Asia.

British power: from mercantilism to free trade

Just as Portugal's colonial empire declined with the growing power of the Netherlands at the beginning of the seventeenth century, so the Dutch in turn gave way before the new colonizing energy of Britain. At the beginning of the eighteenth century Britain benefited from a combination of growing naval power and a vibrant domestic economy, the two fundamental requirements for the development of a successful seaborne empire.

At the beginning of the eighteenth century Britain benefited from a combination of growing naval power and a vibrant domestic economy, the two fundamental requirements for the development of a successful seaborne empire.

Britain's rise among the European colonial powers was not quite as meteoric as that of the Netherlands at the beginning of the seventeenth century. English maritime power had been considerable since the time of Henry VIII, and grew stronger in the Elizabethan age. The second half of the sixteenth century had seen the establishment of the first English colonies in the Caribbean. This was quickly followed by settlements in North America in the first years of the seventeenth century. Sugar from the Caribbean and tobacco and cotton from the Carolinas soon became important parts of the English economy. These developments were not lost on England's neighbours. The Spanish, Dutch and French eyed the extension of England's imperial reach warily. Its closest neighbour, on the other hand, sought to follow England's example. Scotland, still a separate state at the end of the seventeenth century and a relatively impoverished one, tried to carve out a colonial role for itself with the establishment of a settlement at Darièn in the Panama isthmus. It was a completely disastrous undertaking and its economic consequences probably sped the Act of Union with England a few years later.

The plantation production in the English (later British) colonies in the Americas was entirely dependent on the African slave trade. Slavery was hardly a new phenomenon. It had been widely practised within Africa before the arrival of the new Atlantic traders, though it had been largely unknown in Western Europe since the medieval period. Now slavery became a crucial part of the new global economy, illustrating how the colonial project could alter the west European moral landscape. The racism that was inseparable from the great colonizing surge of the late nineteenth century derived in part from the dilemmas of the slave colonialism which preceded it. Attempts in Enlightenment Europe to find a moral rationalization for the slave trade usually ended with the fundamental humanity of the African being questioned – which in turn created a fertile ground for the growth of 'scientific' theories of racial difference.

However weak its moral justification, plantation slavery would continue because, quite simply, successful colonial economies depended on it. This was the age of 'mercantilism'. An economic proposition rather than a theory, mercantilism regarded the tropical colonies first and last as sources of national wealth. The maximum resource had to be extracted from colonial possessions. This could then be converted into bullion which, the mercantilists argued, was the only true measure of a nation's wealth. Slavery was one indispensable means of maximizing colonial productivity for conversion into gold and silver. But the national wealth accrued in this way had to be protected from competition. In England one mechanism for this was the Navigation Acts of 1651 and 1663 which restricted the transport and trade of colonial produce to English vessels. The other weapon in the mercantile protectionist armoury was, of course, state-protected companies. The British East India Company was established in 1600 and, like its Dutch and French counterparts in Asia and the Americas, was designed to exclude other states from the exploitation of national colonial wealth.

Throughout the seventeenth century, when the mercantilist philosophy was dominant, England and the Netherlands were the key competitors in this 'winner-takes-all' game. Spain and Portugal were in long-term decline and France, distracted by domestic preoccupations, was only a tentative colonial power. By the end of this mercantilist century, the game had swung irrevocably in England's favour. With the larger population and resource base and a bigger domestic market than Holland, England entered the eighteenth century as the dominant European colonial power. It was therefore well placed to benefit from the next economic theology that succeeded mercantilism. This was the 'classical economics' of free trade advocated by Adam Smith and David Ricardo. The gradual dismantling of formal protectionism which the classical economists advocated created a world in which countries with a large and productive population, a well-organized and stable financial system and a powerful merchant shipping industry could dominate the colonial project.

The colonial ascendancy of England – or more correctly Britain, after the 1707 Act of Union with Scotland – was also secured by its military superiority in Europe. Throughout the first half of the eighteenth century there was a sequence of wars which, though European in origin, had profound effects on the balance of power in the colonial world. The major conflict, at least in terms of its longer-term consequences, was the Seven Years War fought between 1756 and 1763. In Europe the war was continent-wide, involving Prussia and Britain on one side against France, Austria and Russia on the other. But just as both World Wars of the twentieth century had their colonial battle-fields, so the Seven Years War was also fought out between Britain and France in North America and in India. In both these colonial theatres Britain emerged dominant, a position formalized by the Treaty of Paris which ended the war, and its ascendancy continued into the nineteenth century. France might have been expected to capitalize on the American War of Independence and the emergence of the new United States after Britain's forced decolonization of 1776; indeed it made efforts to do so. But the great convulsion of the French Revolution loomed, and France's imperial reach was sharply reduced at the beginning of the nineteenth century.

The impact of industrialization

While the European colonial powers circled each other in Asia and the Americas in the eighteenth century, deep economic and social changes were under way at home. Beginning in Britain, the dominant economic and imperial power of the time, this transformation soon spread out to the other colonizing countries on the continent. It was to have a profound impact on the future development of European colonialism as a whole. The Industrial

Revolution changed the rules at several different levels of the colonial game. The effects of European industrialization would be felt throughout the existing empires, in colonies of settlement as much as in colonies of exploitation. More importantly, however, industrialization would provide the springboard for Europe's leap into a new unprecedented period of colonial expansion.

The vast increase in manufacturing production in Britain brought by industrialization changed the economic basis of colonialism. Plantation colonies with their dependency on the slave trade became less and less significant to the metropolitan economy. Trade in manufactured goods became increasingly important and eventually it was necessary to develop new colonial spaces to maximize the profit from this. At the same time, access to particular products, notably cotton, became more urgent as the new textile processes which led the Industrial Revolution became ever greedier for raw materials. India therefore took on a new importance as both a supplier of these materials and a consumer of the made products.

This new economic setting also brought a renewed interest in China as a market for manufactured goods. Britain therefore developed a form of 'semi-colonialism' there. In the meantime, the corresponding decline in the economic importance of the Caribbean plantation colonies allowed hitherto closed ears and minds to open to the moral pronouncements of the abolitionists. The Atlantic slave trade was ended by the British Parliament in 1807 and this further speeded the decline of the West Indies within the colonial economy. Colonial investors were now looking elsewhere. The dominant grip that Britain had held on world trade throughout the eighteenth century was hugely strengthened by its pioneering position in the sequence of European Industrial Revolutions. To those that had, would be given, was the guiding tenet of the new gospel of colonial free trade.

Beyond its impact on the economics of empire, the Industrial Revolution also brought social changes to Britain which affected patterns of colonial expansion. Urbanization increased dramatically in Britain at the end of the eighteenth century. One consequence of this was a growing population of urban poor. Emigration provided one way out of this (as, *in extremis*, did criminal transportation) and this gave a new impetus to the development of colonies of settlement in Australasia and North America. The majority of the new town dwellers were not drawn to emigration, of course. Their move from the countryside had often been driven by the new economic opportunities industrialization appeared to offer. Their new environment brought changes to the world view of people whose horizons had previously been, literally, parochial. A new sense of national identity developed, first in Britain and then in the other countries of Western Europe. As the nineteenth century advanced there was a blending of imperial pride with a new and dangerous nationalism which deepened the expansionist mindset across Europe.

As the nineteenth century advanced there was a blending of imperial pride with a new and dangerous nationalism which deepened the expansionist mindset across Europe.

The first phase of industrialization shifted the emphasis of colonialism in line with new economic opportunities and demands. Then, later in the nineteenth century, industrial innovations had far-reaching effects on the *processes* of colonialism. Steam power provided hitherto undreamt of opportunities for colonial transport, both of goods and people. Commercial possibilities were transformed and trade became much more intense. Advances in scientific and manufacturing techniques concentrated new, more destructive and more plentiful weapons in the hands of Europeans. By the early nineteenth century exploration, particularly of the African interior, was already being driven by the Enlightenment spirit of scientific enquiry. Technical innovation now overcame many of the practical obstacles to it. Missionary endeavours, spurred on by a religious evangelism (which was itself a product of the new industrial societies), were served by the advances in transport and communications. These explorers and missionaries were frequently the advance guard of formal colonization.

Up to this point in history, the technological gap between the European colonizer and the colonized of the Americas, Asia or Africa had not really been a wide one. Both sides in the relationship had been dependent on sail-power. Each had confronted the other with weapons of a similar type. The colonizers' monopoly of early firearms was of only limited benefit to them. Now the technological advantage shifted dramatically to the colonizer. This diverging capacity had effects that were more than purely practical. The new sense of European technical superiority inflated underlying attitudes of contempt by the dominant for the dominated, an unvarying characteristic of the colonial relationship.

By the mid-nineteenth century the entire character of European colonialism was changing. And the process of change was accelerating as other west European countries followed

Britain on the path of industrialization. Other powers now positioned themselves to challenge the imperial dominance that Britain had enjoyed for the previous 150 years. A 'new imperialism' was beckoning.

Recommended reading

The state of the global South before the European irruption is explored by Janet Abu-Lughod in *Before European Hegemony: The World System 1250–1350* (London: Oxford University Press, 1989). The generality of the European relationship with the South over the span of the colonial era is the subject of *Europe and the Third World: From Colonialism to Decolonization, c. 1500–1998* (London: Macmillan, 1999) by Bernard Waites. D.K. Fieldhouse covers a narrower chronology in his careful and somewhat conservative study, *The Colonial Empires: A Comparative Study from the Eighteenth Century* (2nd edn, London: Macmillan, 1982).

There are numerous studies of the dominant European imperial powers of the period from the sixteenth century to the eighteenth century. The most celebrated chronicler of the empires of Portugal and Holland, at least in English, is the late Charles Boxer. His two famous accounts are *The Portuguese Seaborne Empire, 1415–1825* (London: Hutchinson, 1969) and *The Dutch Seaborne Empire, 1600–1800* (London: Hutchinson, 1965). Britain is dealt with, perhaps less enduringly, in Niall Ferguson's *Empire: How Britain Made the Modern World* (London: Penguin, 2004). Though contentious in its approach and conclusions (which lie on the right of the political spectrum), Ferguson's book is nevertheless a stimulating read. Also very readable, though less provoking, is Hugh Thomas's *Rivers of Gold: The Rise of the Spanish Empire* (London: Phoenix, 2004).

CHAPTER 2

The 'new imperialism': colonialism to the First World War

WHAT WAS NEW about the 'new imperialism' of the nineteenth century? In many ways, it could be argued, not all that much. Yes, industrialization altered the economic nature of colonialism. It also changed the social setting in which it was pursued. By opening a technological gap between colonizer and colonized, both the processes and the social relations of colonialism had changed. But it is possible to see these as incremental rather than funda-mental transformations. Mercantilism, after all, had given way to free-trade imperialism without bringing a basic change in how European power was exercised overseas. Colonial powers had gained and lost dominance over the previous four centuries, and the geographical focus of colonization had changed frequently without altering the general tempo of the enterprise. However, the striking feature of the new imperialism was the extent and rapidity of change across all aspects of the colonial venture.

The sheer pace and range of expansion was breathtaking. In the thirty years before the First World War, an average of around 600,000 square kilometres of the global South was colonized annually by the global North. At the end of this period Europe controlled the major part of the earth's surface. Much of this was acquired through the so-called scramble for Africa. This added the huge landmass of the continent below the Sahara to a colonial swag-bag already loaded with the Asian and American possessions taken in earlier centuries. In addition, the new imperialism saw the geographical reach of the colonizers extend much further than previously into the Asia-Pacific region. By 1900 colonial rule had already been imposed on 90 per cent of Africa, more than half of Asia and almost the totality of the South Pacific. More than a quarter of the Americas remained under colonial rule despite the disintegration of Spanish and Portuguese power there over the previous century.

The other feature of the time was the dramatic growth in the list of would-be colonizers. The narrative from the fifteenth century had been one of relatively few European colonial powers succeeding each other at the top of an imperial hierarchy. Spain

Region	Percentage under Colonial Rule
Africa	90.4
Asia	56.5
Pacific	98.9
Americas	27.2

The colonial world in 1900

Source: After Alexander Supan, *Die Territoriale Entwicklung der Europäischen Kolonien* (Gotha: Perthes, 1906, p. 254).

and Portugal gave way to the Netherlands, which in turn gave way to Britain, which managed to fight off challenges from France. But by the end of the nineteenth century the stage had become more crowded. Moreover, dangerously, there was no clear hierarchy among the actors. While Britain remained the largest colonial power in terms of the area of its possessions and the size of its imperial population, rivals milled around, challenging both British dominance and each other. The ambitions of the old colonial powers were reinvigorated in the second half of the nineteenth century. To varying degrees France, the Netherlands, Spain and Portugal all rediscovered their imperial vocations. Portugal in particular inaugurated its Third Empire on the basis of its notionally huge (though barely occupied) African territories. But in addition wholly new players arrived on the scene as well. Germany, Belgium, Italy, Japan and the United States all acquired tropical possessions in the years around the turn of the twentieth century.

> *Germany, Belgium, Italy, Japan and the United States all acquired tropical possessions in the years around the turn of the twentieth century.*

Theorizing colonialism

The driving forces of the new imperialism became the subject of intense debate at the beginning of the twentieth century. Scholars and ideologues (categories that were sometimes difficult to separate) argued long and hard. Competing theories claimed to provide a comprehensive explanation of colonialism. In part, this sort of intellectualization was simply a feature of the age that gave birth to the 'new' social sciences. Beyond this,

	Britain	France	Belgium	Netherlands	Germany
Area (1,000 km²)	243.5	550.6	30.6	34.2	543.9
Population (millions)	45.4	42.0	8.3	8.5	67.5
Area of colonies (1,000 km²)	33929	11137	2435	2046	2849
Population of colonies (millions)	470	65	13	66	13

European colonial empires in 1939 (Germany 1914)
Source: After Mary Evelyn Townsend, *European Colonial Expansion since 1871* (Chicago: Lippincott, 1941, p. 19).

Europe was in a state of unprecedented ideological ferment at this time. Throughout the continent, monarchism confronted liberalism, which in turn clashed with social democracy. Further to the left lay the new and seductive claims of Marxism. Inevitably, all of the main political perspectives had something to say about colonialism and its place in the general battle of ideas.

In one sense there was an obvious explanatory 'theory' of the new surge of colonialism: it happened because it *could* happen. Industrialization had created the technological wherewithal that allowed the more industrially advanced states to project their power as never before. Colonies became one of the basic currencies of national prestige within the international hierarchy. But while this was undoubtedly a background factor, other explanations were advanced that had less to do with national psychology and more to do with hard economics. These too took as their starting point the consequences of industrialization.

Economics: colonialism and European capitalism

Two names dominate the economic analysis of imperialism at the beginning of the twentieth century: John A. Hobson and Vladimir Ilyich Lenin. Although the first was an English liberal journalist and economist, and the

Two names dominate the economic analysis of imperialism at the beginning of the twentieth century: John A. Hobson and Vladimir Ilyich Lenin.

second a Russian revolutionary, their respective theories were in fact strikingly similar. Hobson's work, published in 1902, was read and digested by Lenin whose own theory appeared fourteen years later during the First World War. Both theories saw the particular stage reached by advanced capitalism at the end of the nineteenth century as the key factor driving the sudden expansion of colonial acquisition.

John A. Hobson (1858–1940)

Hobson came from a prosperous provincial newspaper family, a background that shaped his future as a journalist and social commentator. After graduating from Oxford he became a schoolteacher. With his move to London in 1887, however, the contours of his later work began to emerge. The swirl of social and political ideas which he encountered in the salons of the capital in the last years of the nineteenth century encouraged the development of his world view. A fast and prolific writer, he became a spokesman for the 'new liberalism' of the time, a doctrine distinguished by its concern with social conditions and the ethics of political behaviour (in contrast to the traditional liberal preoccupations with economic and personal freedom). His view of colonialism, set out in his 1902 work *Imperialism: a Study*, was characteristically as much a call for reform as an explanatory theory. Imperialism, he argued, was the inevitable (and undesirable) result of low wages and overproduction at home. Unable to find a market for the abundance of goods produced in Europe, industry sought out new markets and new investment opportunities in the colonies. The 'problem' of imperialism could therefore be 'solved' through higher purchasing power (wages) at home. His general view of imperialism fundamentally shaped the thinking of Lenin. Hobson had less influence on academic economists at home, who tended to dismiss his ideas as 'journalistic'. Although in later life his beliefs took him from the Liberal to the Labour Party, he was uncomfortable with Labour's roots in industrial trade unionism. Hobson died just after the outbreak of the Second Word War, a dark time for the passing of an inveterate social and political optimist.

Hobson's book, *Imperialism: a Study*, grew out of his opposition to the Boer War in South Africa. In his view, widely shared among liberal opinion in England at the time, the war was being fought by Britain's army on behalf of self-seeking financial interests, whatever the patriotic arguments to the contrary. The purpose of the war, Hobson believed, was to gain control of South Africa for a new breed of colonial capitalists greedy for its mineral wealth. The main obstacles to this were the Dutch-descended Boers who were mainly farmers and who resisted the advance of this modern sector. Therefore a change in political control in South Africa had to be engineered in the interests of capitalist exploitation. From this specific injustice, Hobson argued, it was possible to glimpse the underlying dynamics of contemporary colonialism as a whole. In a number of important senses, he pointed out, imperialism did not make good political sense. As a national policy it was expensive and troublesome. Its economic returns to the nation were less than the outlay of state resources necessary to acquire and hold overseas possessions. The driving force, therefore, was not the national interest in any conventional sense, but the demands of national economies which had been distorted by the process of rapid industrialization.

The breakneck pace of capitalist growth in the nineteenth century had produced three interrelated conditions. Together, these impelled states towards colonialism. First, industrialization had led to the overproduction of goods. Domestic markets were becoming over-supplied and glutted. As a result, capitalist profits were put in jeopardy. This massively expanded production need not be a problem in itself. With sufficiently buoyant domestic consumption it could be absorbed. But here the second condition came into play. The wages of the industrial workers whose labour drove this over-production were too low to permit them to consume the surplus and thus rebalance the economy. Instead, and this was the third leg of the stool which supported colonialism, faced with the low profits created by these conditions, the capitalists preferred to accumulate their returns rather than reinvest them in the apparently unproductive domestic economy.

This accumulated capital became like fermenting liquor in a poorly corked bottle. It naturally sought to break out in new directions which would provide profits unavailable at home. The result was economic adventurism which took European capitalism beyond the moribund domestic market and into the colonies. Governments in the meantime, in thrall to the power of capitalism, felt obliged to provide the policies and means to facilitate this. The 'new imperialism', Hobson wrote,

differs from the older, first, in substituting for the ambition of a single growing empire the theory and the practice of competing empires, each motivated by similar lusts of political aggrandizement and commercial gain; secondly, in the dominance of financial or investing over mercantile interests

(*J.A. Hobson, Imperialism: a Study [1902], p. 324*)

Imperialism was not about national commerce and trade, in other words, but about the competitive search for new sources of profit for decaying capital.

Lenin, although writing from a radically different ideological perspective, differed from Hobson only in detail and, more crucially, in his prescriptions. Published in 1916, *Imperialism: the Highest Stage of Capitalism* argued that the First World War, which was then at its height, was a consequence of imperialism. The conflict was the end point of capitalism, of which imperialism was the highest (in the sense of 'final') phase. Lenin's theory of colonialism is particularly significant because it became the 'orthodox' Marxist explanation which Karl Marx himself had failed to provide. So far as he referred to colonialism at all in his writings, Marx was reasonably well disposed towards it. He produced most of his major work in the mid-nineteenth century, before the great spurt of colonization that came with the 'new imperialism'. For Marx himself, therefore, imperialism was not the pressing issue it had become by Lenin's time.

Vladimir Ilyich Lenin (1870–1924)

Lenin was born into the middle-class, politically sophisticated Ulyanov family in Simbirsk on the River Volga (he adopted the name 'Lenin' only in 1901). When he was seven his brother Alexander was executed for conspiring to assassinate the Czar, and from his teenage years Lenin himself was a committed radical. Although graduating as a lawyer in 1892, he never practised, spending his entire life as a revolutionary agitator and, finally, leader of the Soviet Union. He passed the period from 1896 to 1900 either in prison or in internal exile in Siberia. On his release he travelled to Western Europe and until the October Revolution of 1917 he spent only short periods in Russia, passing his exile writing and organizing from abroad, principally in Switzerland. It was here that in 1916 he wrote his extended essay on colonialism, *Imperialism: the Highest Stage of Capitalism*. He was influenced by the argument of the English writer J.A. Hobson that imperialism was a product of capitalist over-production. Lenin, however, departed from Hobson's reformist prescriptions, insisting that imperialism marked the culminating point of capitalism and was the prelude to socialist revolution. In 1917 he returned to Russia after the abdication of the Czar and the installation of a reformist government. His own 'Bolsheviks' seized power in October 1917, in large part because of their commitment to extracting Russia from the First World War. Lenin guided the infant Soviet Union through the ensuing revolutionary process and civil war. In 1922 he suffered the first of a series of strokes which would eventually kill him in 1924. He was succeeded, against his own warnings, by Joseph Stalin.

Marx viewed British colonialism in Ireland and in India, for example, as an agent of economic and social progress. However strange this may sound to contemporary ears, there was a (Marxist) logic to it. The 'historical materialism' that underlies all Marxist theory requires that societies pass through prescribed phases on the way to communism. Feudalism gives way to capitalism, which in turn succumbs to socialism, which evolves into stateless communism. Anything that accelerates this process is therefore progressive. If colonialism imported capitalism to feudal or even pre-feudal societies then they would arrive on the sunny uplands of communism all the sooner. As colonialism underwent the dramatic changes of pace and range of the late nineteenth century, however, a 'Marxist' theory more attuned to contemporary economic realities seemed to be called for. Lenin stepped forward to provide it.

Like Hobson, Lenin argued that capitalism, having reached a critical stage, was 'driven' towards colonialism. Instead of investing and reinvesting capital at home, because of dwindling profits 'finance capital' was allowed to build up. This finance capital became an accumulation of funds under the control of a few monopolies in search of profitable investment. In other words, capitalism outgrew the territorial limits of its 'home' country. Colonialism offered a protected outlet for this capital. The opportunity was threefold. The colonies were starting from scratch and therefore provided investment opportunities in infrastructural developments like railways and ports. These opportunities were available during the first phase of industrialization in Europe but were now exhausted there. Secondly, the colonies provided an outlet for European products which were not profitable on the home market. Finally, the colonies were a source of raw materials, like rubber, ores and oil, which could feed metropolitan industries and help keep the costs of production low.

Ultimately, Lenin argued, capitalism could not be rescued by colonialism. At best it could be provided with a temporary reprieve. There was no way back, and colonialism was merely a siren voice leading capitalism to its doom rather than its salvation. The world is finite, and the inexorable growth of competing national capitalisms beyond national frontiers must eventually lead to collision and conflict. In the Marxist view the state was merely an executive committee of the dominant economic class. When that class was a capitalist one, the

In the Marxist view the state was merely an executive committee of the dominant economic class.

state would act in the interest of capitalism as perceived by capitalists. Eventually this misguided capitalism would lead to international conflict and mutual self-destruction.

When first presented, Lenin's ideas were persuasive. After all, an apocalyptic world war was taking place between advanced capitalist states following an intensive period of colonial rivalry. Subsequent events seemed to validate further Lenin's arguments. The Bolshevik revolution in Russia in 1917, and the rash of communist uprisings in central Europe that followed it after the end of the war, seemed to suggest that the transition from the last stage of capitalism to socialism was indeed under way. Hobson, on the other hand, saw another way forward. However similar to Lenin's his diagnosis of the ills of colonialism might be, he believed the situation could be remedied within the existing economic system. The three-headed monster of over-production, low wages and over-saving could be tamed. With higher wages European workers would have the purchasing power to create a domestic market that could absorb high levels of production. This in turn would transform the domestic investment situation by providing opportunities for profits at home.

The vicious circle would therefore be transformed into a virtuous one and the grounds for aggressive colonialism would disappear. To Lenin this optimistic prognosis merely confirmed Hobson's roots in liberal reformism.

In fact, neither prescription proved valid. Colonization continued, though at a slower rate as the territorial opportunities naturally diminished. It was far from clear in any case that colonial expansion was the product of monopoly capitalism. Capitalism at the beginning of the twentieth century may not have been at the point Hobson and Lenin supposed. In reality there were few obvious commercial opportunities in most of the territory occupied by European colonialists at the time of the new imperialism. Investment in Africa and the Pacific carried high risks and few guarantees of returns. West European funds had many other outlets in the world beyond the recently acquired tropical possessions. Trade, it seemed, did not follow the flag in the way suggested by imperial enthusiasts. By 1913, on the eve of the supposed great imperialist war, 80 per cent of British and French trade and 90 per cent of that of Germany was with other European countries or areas long settled by Europeans. To the extent that capital did go to 'non-European' destinations it was to Latin America and Asiatic Russia, areas that may have lagged behind in development but which were not in any formal sense colonies. Capitalism, far from destroying itself in the war of 1914–18, re-emerged to grow stronger than ever over the coming century.

Social explanations: colonialism as 'atavism'

The state of capitalism and its impact on the world economy was not the only explanation for colonialism on offer at the beginning of the twentieth century. A range of sociological and cultural theories emerged from the newly influential social sciences.

In 1919 the liberal Austrian sociologist Joseph Schumpeter proposed an intriguing non-economic theory in two influential articles called 'The Sociology of Imperialism', published in the German language journal *Archive of Social Science and Social Policy*. While not dismissing the significance of economics (Schumpeter himself had been an economist), he suggested that the root causes of colonial expansion lie deeper in human history than transitory economic cycles. His starting point was to argue that colonialism, far from providing even a temporary refuge for capitalism, was utterly irrational in economic terms. It had no tangible material benefit to the imperial power. It drained resources away from the development of prosperous, modern economies into military adventures which brought no meaningful economic return. Instead, Schumpeter argued, colonialism was the result of a 'natural' disposition on the part of the state to expand its own territory.

This, of course, directly contradicted the arguments of Hobson and Lenin who saw colonialism as primarily an economic activity, however illusory its long-term benefits might be. In Schumpeter's view, the appeal of colonialism lay deeper, in the darker recesses of human experience where a propensity had developed for conflict and conquest. This was not a human instinct in the sense that his Viennese

> *In Schumpeter's view, the appeal of colonialism lay deeper, in the darker recesses of human experience where a propensity had developed for conflict and conquest.*

contemporary Sigmund Freud would have understood it. It was 'learned' behaviour dating from a distant past when a dominant warrior caste protected communities from destruction. Modern societies, Schumpeter suggested, have 'atavistic' – backward-looking – tendencies. As a result, social forces that in rational terms are utterly anachronistic continue to determine social and political action. While modern states and societies might produce political and economic elites attuned to the realities of the contemporary world, their counterparts in the military had fundamentally different (atavistic) perspectives.

Military leaders in nineteenth- and early twentieth-century Europe came almost exclusively from conservative aristocratic families. Their personal and professional world view was still shaped by antique warrior attitudes about national prestige and honour. As Schumpeter saw it, they were committed to imperial conquest not because of any rational advantage it might bring, but simply because they were, to use a modern idiom, 'programmed' for it. Reluctant to confront this section of the ruling class (which, though backward-looking, was by its very nature still immensely powerful), policy makers tended to indulge its taste for colonial adventurism, however much that went against the real interests of the modern state.

Beyond Schumpeter's specific theory, the argument that European governments were driven against their better judgement into pursuing colonial policies is a common one. Hobson and Lenin in their different ways saw governments (or 'the state') as willing accomplices of self-seeking capitalism. To Hobson this was misguided policy, while for Lenin it was merely inevitable because it was the central purpose of the state under capitalism to pursue the interest of capitalism. But there is another image of state complicity – that of the harassed policy maker manoeuvred into colonial adventures by facts created on the ground by others. These might be the result of the good intentions of missionaries and humanitarians or the more self-serving schemes of settlers and traders, but, either way, the state was pulled into line behind these informal forces. Arguably, much of Britain's advance into central and southern Africa in the second half of the nineteenth century came about in this way rather than as rational and planned policy. Certainly, Otto von Bismarck was deeply reluctant to permit Germany to enter the colonial game during his time in power. A German overseas empire was seen by many of his countrymen as the ultimate affirmation of newly unified Germany's status as a great power. For Bismarck, the wily master of realpolitik, it was a dangerous vanity.

The 'civilizing mission': colonialism as cultural superiority

The grand theorists of imperialism have tended to dismiss the idea of varied and unmeasurable pressures on policy makers. For Marxists in particular such a haphazard narrative of colonialism runs against their view of historical narrative as a predetermined scheme. In their intellectual universe it is the great tectonic movements in world history that determine events like the new imperialism. Those like Schumpeter who proposed overarching sociological theories also have little time for accounts that see colonialism as the produce of more haphazard forces. However, the consequences of social and cultural conditions at particular times and places cannot simply be discounted. At the end of the nineteenth century, for example, the idea of a 'civilizing mission' to the less favoured races overseas was a real and potent force in shaping public attitudes towards colonialism. Whether religious or secular in inspiration, whether self-aggrandizing or altruistic in its intentions, the idea that colonization was in a real sense a 'duty' was widespread and influential.

Where did this mindset come from? Like so much connected with colonialism at this time it was a product – albeit an indirect one – of industrialization. The industrial revolution in Europe dramatically widened the technological distance between col-onizer and colonized. It altered fundamentally the terms of the colonial relationship. Technological advance first gave rise to – and then was driven on by – a cult of progress. Europeans (and North Americans) developed a great conceit of themselves in relation to the rest of the world, based on their apparently limit-less capacity for 'improvement'.

Other things followed in the train of this. Social mores changed in Europe. A much wider portion of the populations of industrializing European countries became preoccupied with social reputation and 'respectability'. This further increased the sense of social and cultural superiority on the part of the colonizer towards the 'untamed savages' being colonized. The new sensibility of respectable godliness went hand-in-hand with religious revival. An interest in Christian evangelism followed the social dislocation of industrialization in many European countries. The mis-

An interest in Christian evangelism followed the social dislocation of industrialization in many European countries.

sionary urge was not projected exclusively on to the colonies at this time, of course. Campaigns to improve the lot of the domestic poor and wayward were also a feature of the high Victorian and Edwardian periods in Britain and grew from the same social mindset. The gifts and virtues bestowed by providence on the respectable middle classes could surely, with sufficient effort, be imposed on others, whether in the slums of the new industrial cities or across the benighted plains of Africa.

This was the basis of the civilizing mission as conceived in Britain at least. Other European colonialisms offered variations. The French had their own *mission civilisatrice*. This took its inspiration from the secular rationalism of the Napoleonic era rather than the evangelism of nineteenth-century Anglicanism or Scottish Presbyterianism. Having tried with limited success at the end of the eighteenth century to implant the social and intellectual virtues of its revolution in its European neighbours, France now sought to impose them on new subjects in the tropics. The underlying assumptions of both the British and the French variants of the civilizing mission were essentially the same, however. Colonization was, above all, a 'white man's burden' to be borne with fortitude and self-sacrifice by the superior race.

Rudyard Kipling's poem of 1899, which brought the phrase into common usage, distils this world view:

Take up the White Man's burden
Send forth the best ye breed
Go bind your sons to exile
To serve your captives' need;
To wait in heavy harness,

On fluttered folk and wild
Your new-caught, sullen peoples,
Half-devil and half-child.

The poem was written soon after the seizure of the Philippines from Spain by the United States and was directed to the masters of the new imperial project. Colonialism was portrayed here not merely as a self-sacrificial act of altruism but as a joint enterprise by the white races united in service rather than divided by imperial rivalry:

Take up the White Man's burden
Have done with childish days
The lightly proffered laurel,
The easy, ungrudged praise.
Comes now, to search your manhood
Through all the thankless years
Cold, edged with dear-bought wisdom,
The judgment of your peers!

It was nothing less than a welcome address to a new initiate of a sacred order. Whatever was happening down in the engine-room of the world economy, for millions across Europe where public opinion was a newly emerging political force, the sense of cultural mission was on its own a sufficient justification for the colonial project.

Global strategy: colonialism as a 'security dilemma'

There were many later elaborations on these contemporary theories of colonialism. Economic explanations in particular became the subject of almost theological debate among Marxists and non-Marxists alike as it became clear that, whatever Lenin's conviction, the collapse of capitalism had not come about after the 'imperialist' war of 1914–18. Much later a revised Marxism would dominate the debates about neocolonialism that emerged in the 1970s in the aftermath of decolonization. In the intervening period, though, another interpretation was offered, one that deserves attention not least because it connects with contemporary theories of international relations.

In 1953 two English historians, Ronald Robinson and John Gallagher, published an article in the *English Historical Review* with the title 'The Imperialism of Free Trade'. Their argument, based on a close reading of British government documents, was that there was really no such thing as the 'new imperialism', merely an intensification of what had already been going on. Britain at least, they argued, remained committed to the free-trade precepts of the eighteenth century. The apparent changes of the nineteenth century were in essence manoeuvres designed to secure that free trade, particularly with the older European possessions in Asia. The pair expanded and developed this argument in 1961 when they published their influential book, *Africa and the Victorians: the Official Mind of Imperialism*. Here colonialism in Africa was presented as primarily strategic, though admittedly still at the service of those older economic interests. Britain was anxious to secure Egypt because of its trading interests in the southern Mediterranean. But Egypt's interest for British imperi-

> *Britain was anxious to secure Egypt because of its trading interests in the southern Mediterranean.*

alism grew spectacularly in the second half of the nineteenth century with the opening of the Suez Canal. This offered new rapid access for Europe to the Middle East and Asia. The Cape of Good Hope, at the other end of Africa, was already important for imperialism for the same reason, particularly in relation to the efficiency of trade routes to India.

British governments undertook colonial ventures into the interior of Africa only reluctantly, according to Robinson and Gallagher. These undertakings were secondary to the securing of the key strategic points at the top and bottom of the continent. They became necessary, however, because the activities of other, newer colonialists created uncertainty and threatened the stable functioning of the free-trade colonialism established in the eighteenth century. The surge of colonization in the late nine-teenth century therefore was about the 'preclusion' of sources of instability. Problems that could disturb the steady tenor of existing colonial interests had to be pre-empted. Colonialism was not, as Hobson and Lenin argued, a new economic phenom-enon. The lack of any real evidence of investment in Europe's new African possessions was called in evidence of this. The new imperialism, in short, was not driven by a new economic compe-tition; it was designed to preserve an existing one.

In this strategic view Britain and its apparent colonial rivals faced what in the contemporary language of international theory would be a 'security dilemma'. A threat (instability) is perceived when another imperial country shows interest in territory adja-cent to an established colony. This created a dilemma for policy makers. Should action (a new preclusive colonial occupation) be taken to meet this threat? When this response does take place, far from stabilizing the situation, it provokes another cycle of threat perception among rival actors who now face their own security dilemma. Consequently, they take what they regard as appropriate action – in the form of further colonial occupation. And so on. The idea of a security dilemma is central to neo-realist theory in International Relations. This places national power at the centre of interaction between states but, unlike traditional explanations of power politics, blames the resulting conflict on the nature of the system rather than the malign nature of states. Even with the best of intentions states, when required to look after their national interests within an unregulated system, will face security dilemmas and will react to them in ways that tend to escalate tension and competition. From this perspective it is not difficult to see the colonial scramble of the late nineteenth and early twentieth centuries less as an avaricious land-grab than as a sequence of defensive reactions to (mis)perceived threats. It is easy to understand how this cycle of behaviour in the distant tropics will eventually return to destabilize European international relations at their geographic centre.

A theory of everything?

Much intellectual energy has been expended over the past century in the struggle to 'prove' one true comprehensive theory of colonialism. It has been energy misspent; there is none. This is not, as ideologues would insist, an evasion; it is simply the common sense response to the wealth of convincing arguments deployed across the range of explanations on offer, Marxist and non-Marxist, economic and non-economic, schematic and haphazard. There is no intellectual law that makes competing theories mutually exclusive. If postmodernism has made any valid contribution to contemporary thought, it lies in its rejection of overarching narratives that claim to provide single-cause explanations of complex social phenomena.

Certainly, there had been rapid and far-reaching technological innovation in Western Europe, but there is no reason to suppose that this on its own initiated the new surge of colonization, though it may have encouraged it. Yes, things were happening to international capitalism at the end of the nineteenth century which must have had an impact on colonial policy, but that is far from proof that capitalism determined and controlled colonization. There were also fundamental social changes taking place in Western Europe and the United States at this time. Political systems were changing and with them their controlling elites. Again, this must have had an influence on colonial policy. Moreover, European populations had acquired a greater sense of racial and national superiority that both drove the competitive aspects of colonialism and provided it with a cultural justification. But, again, it is unlikely that this would be sufficient to determine the whole process of colonization. Nor were the strategic concerns of imperial countries anxious to preserve older colonial benefits. These worries were no doubt a factor in the larger canvas of colonialism. But while probably playing a role in the scramble for Africa, they had little significance, say, in the South Pacific where the process of colonization was just as frenetic in the second half of the nineteenth century. In short, therefore, there were many elements that converged in the immensely complex and multi-stranded processes of the new imperialism, but none was *the* single controlling factor.

Colonial rivalry, the international system and the First World War

Cause or symptom – was the First World War the inevitable consequence of the spurt of colonial adventurism that preceded it? Or was colonialism merely a side-effect of an international system which was in any case on a downward spiral to collapse? Some of the theories just considered would see colonialism as a major cause of the conflict. For Lenin the war was a predetermined consequence of imperialism. It would, he argued, prove a watershed, heralding the replacement of capitalism with socialism. The deep militaristic urges that Schumpeter claimed drove imperial expansion might also be seen in the war fever that overtook Europe in 1914. Similarly, the logic of the 'security dilemma' – the cycle of threat perception and reaction into which the European colonial powers had drifted at the beginning of the twentieth century – would also suggest that war was a consequence of the colonial scramble.

Nationalism in the Balkans and Eastern Europe, territorial tensions between Germany and France, and a reckless naval race between Britain and Germany already seemed to make the outbreak of a major war likely at this time.

Yet, when the focus is widened to place colonialism against the other pressures building in the system in the years leading up to 1914, it seems a less significant element. 'Imperialism' may indeed have been the major cause of the conflict, but not the 'new imperialism' of the decades before 1914. The four great continental empires –

Hapsburg Austria, Hohenzollern Germany, Ottoman Turkey and Romanov Russia – had more than enough issues among them in Europe without having to look to the tropics for reasons to fight each other. Nationalism in the Balkans and Eastern Europe, territorial tensions between Germany and France, and a reckless naval race between Britain and Germany already seemed to make the outbreak of a major war likely at this time.

Against this background it is possible to argue that, far from being an unregulated, sharp-elbowed jostle for territory, the process of colonization and the international relations around it were rather well managed in comparison with seething enmities festering elsewhere in the system. The Berlin conference on West Africa in 1884–85 was an early example of a type of multilateral diplomacy that would become common in the next century. At Berlin the European colonial powers and the United States (in the absence, needless to say, of any African representation) met to agree spheres of influence and lay down rules for the acquisition of territory. The conference took place at a critical phase of European expansion in sub-Saharan Africa. It was in effect a recognition that the plunder of the continent should be conducted with due care for the mutual interest of the plunderers rather than as an unbridled land-grab. In most respects, the Berlin process was successful. A general template was established within which Britain, France, Germany, Italy and Portugal all reached agreements among themselves on the development of their colonial empires in Africa over the next fifteen years.

There were colonial conflicts, certainly. The worst of these, at least in relation to pre-war diplomacy, were the two 'Moroccan crises' of 1905–06 and 1911–12. These derived from the ambitions of a new assertive Germany in North Africa, which conflicted with existing French influence there. Both were resolved in France's favour when Germany's (literal) gunboat diplomacy failed to intimidate. The second confrontation was particularly dangerous, as German warship movements around the port of Agadir pushed the Anglo-German naval race to the foreground. Claims that the incident brought Europe to the verge of war are exaggerated, however. So too was the supposed threat to peace caused by Germany's support for the Boers in South Africa in the 1890s. The German position there was rhetorical and mischievous rather than threatening in any concrete sense. The conflict was settled, moreover, many years before the outbreak of hostilities in 1914.

Other colonial confrontations, far from hardening the battle lines of the First World War, involved rivalries between countries that would later be bound together as wartime allies. A general war was predicted over the clash between Britain and France in 1898 at Fashoda in southern Sudan. Here French ambitions to establish a geographically continuous presence across Africa on an east–west axis (linking its equatorial colonies in the west with its possessions in the north and on the southern Mediterranean coast) literally cut across Britain's north–south, Cairo to the Cape plans. Although the crisis was a major one in diplomatic terms, France withdrew before there was any real prospect of a significant outbreak of hostilities.

Eight years earlier, in very similar circumstances, Portugal had been forced to abandon its own transcontinental plans in the face of a British ultimatum. Lisbon's idea had been to link its two southern African colonies, Mozambique and Angola, to give it possession of a single band of Africa from the Indian Ocean to the Atlantic. This too, however, was incompatible with Britain's north–south axis. With some additional pressure from the missionary successors of David Livingstone in the disputed territory, a British ultimatum in 1890 ended Portugal's great imperial dream. Yet, here also there was no long-term damage done to diplomacy inside Europe. Far from translating its grudge into war in Europe, Portugal, like France, would eventually ally itself with Britain in the First World War.

The striking thing about colonial confrontations then was not that they occurred but that they occurred so rarely – and were as likely to be between future allies as enemies. Finally, even where there is a trail to be traced between colonial conflict and the divisions of 1914–18, there is little real evidence in retrospect that the situation was truly critical to peace. Agadir, in short, was not Sarajevo, nor ever likely to be. What is beyond dispute, however, is that the *consequence* of the First World War, if not its cause, was of huge significance for colonialism. After 1918 the political environment in which colonial relations were conducted changed completely.

Recommended reading

The original theories of imperialism of J.A. Hobson and V.I. Lenin are available in (relatively) modern editions – respectively: *Imperialism: A Study* (London: Unwin Hyman, 1988) and *Imperialism: The Highest Stage of Capitalism* (London: Pluto, 1996). The more political, 'preclusive' explanation of the new imperialism offered by Ronald Robinson and John Gallagher can be found in their *Africa and the Victorians: The Official Mind of Imperialism* (London: Macmillan, 1961).

Secondary studies of the theories of the new imperialism can be found in Roger Owen and Bob Sutcliffe (eds), *Studies in the*

Theory of Imperialism (London: Longman, 1972). The debate around the Robinson and Gallagher thesis is explored in a book edited by William Roger Louis, *Imperialism: The Robinson and Gallagher Controversy* (New York: New Viewpoints, 1976).

The generality of Europe's new imperialism is dealt with by A.N. Porter in *European Imperialism, 1860–1914* (London: Palgrave, 1995) and in Thomas Packenham's *The Scramble for Africa* (London: Abacus, 1992).

There are numerous studies of British colonialism during this period. Volume III of the *Oxford History of the British Empire* edited by Judith Brown and William Roger Louis, *The Nineteenth Century* (London: Oxford University Press, 1999), is as comprehensive as might be expected. Bernard Porter's *The Lion's Share: A Short History of British Imperialism, 1850–1983* (London: Longman, 1984) covers the ground in more concise and accessible form.

The French empire of the nineteenth and twentieth century is dealt with in Robert Aldrich's stimulating book *Greater France: A Short History of French Overseas Expansion* (London: Palgrave, 1996) and by Susan Bayly in *The French Empire, 1830–1962* (London: Longman, 2000). The horrors of Belgium's exploitative colonization of the Congo is the subject of Adam Hochschild's highly readable *King Leopold's Ghost: A Story of Greed, Terror and Heroism* (London: Pan, 2006). Portugal is dealt with in a more conventional – though still stimulating – way by Gervaise Clarence-Smith in *The Third Portuguese Empire, 1825–1975: A Study in Economic Imperialism* (Manchester: Manchester University Press, 1985). The relatively short episode of German tropical colonialism is the subject of a book by Sara Friedrichsmayer and others: *The Imperialist Imagination: German Colonialism and its Legacy* (Ann Arbor: Michigan University Press, 1998).

The ambivalent position of the United States towards colonialism is the subject of *The United States and Imperialism* (Oxford: Blackwell, 2001) by Frank A. Ninkovich and *The Forging of the American Empire: A History of American Imperialism from the Revolution to Vietnam* (London: Pluto, 2003) by Sidney Lens.

CHAPTER 3

The interwar years: colonialism in question

THE FIRST WORLD WAR brought the end of the old internal European empires of Austria, Germany, Russia and Turkey. A new post-imperial map of Europe emerged with novel divisions and names, Yugoslavia and Czechoslovakia among them. Between many existing states borders were altered, sometimes dramatically. France, Germany and Poland all looked very different from five years previously. The years following the war also saw a clear constitutional break between Britain and its white dominions of Canada, South Africa, Australia and New Zealand. Although still bound to Britain in the new Commonwealth – and by obvious ties of sentiment between the rulers of the settler regimes and their country of origin – the status of these territories as sovereign states was confirmed by the Statute of Westminster in 1931. In the meantime, Ireland (or at least twenty-six of its thirty-two counties) had achieved statehood in 1921 after a war of independence. This, however, was to prove a botched decolonization that would haunt relations between Ireland and Britain into the twenty-first century.

The post-imperial transformation within Europe itself in these years had been dramatic, but there was little sign that this continental 'decolonization' affected European thinking about the colonial empires in the tropics. Self-determination for European neighbours, however peculiar their cultures and however savage their politics, was of a totally different order from the situation in far-flung empires on which the sun never set. Independence for European migrant regimes like those of the white Commonwealth was not only inevitable, in the view of even the most committed imperialist, but right and proper as well. Contemplating any fundamental change in 'African Africa' or 'Asian Asia' was on the other hand quite a different prospect.

Despite this, the connection between what had become widely accepted rights of Europeans to self-determination and the continuation of colonial rule elsewhere was now being made among the populations of the tropical empires themselves. The vanguard of this was to be found among those colonial subjects conscripted to serve in the armies of the metropolitan powers. British and French colonial troops, mainly from India and North Africa, shared the horrors of the war in all of its major theatres. Awareness of the gulf between the rhetoric of self-determination and democracy deployed by the European powers, and the continuing servitude of their colonies was kindled in the First World War, though it would be in the next one that it would fully catch flame. Undoubtedly too, the towering confidence in their own power and capacity exuded by European imperial states in 1914 could not survive the horrors of the trenches intact. But the general reaction among the European victors was to avoid too much morbid contemplation and to seek comfort in a return to pre-war certainties – among which imperial pomp was prominent.

In this fragile climate uncomfortable questions about the future of colonialism were posed more pressingly by the United States than Europe itself. The war had to all intents and purposes been won for the allies by the intervention of the United States in 1917. Without this, the bloody stalemate on the western front might just as easily have resolved itself in Germany's favour and the history of the twentieth century could have taken a dramatically different path. As it was, the United States was left at the end of 1918 with extremely powerful cards to play at the peace conferences.

The war had to all intents and purposes been won for the allies by the intervention of the United States in 1917.

These cards were in the hands of the Democrat president, Woodrow Wilson. The son of a Presbyterian minister and, before entering politics full-time, a distinguished academic, Wilson seemed to personify probity and moral purpose. He persuaded Congress to overcome its reluctance to enter the war largely by presenting the venture as a sacred responsibility. His arguments were summed up in the famous Fourteen Points of January 1918 which outlined US war aims. These were deeply rooted in an ethical view of America's responsibilities to the world. The fifth of the points called for a 'free, open-minded, and absolutely impartial adjustment of all colonial claims, based upon a strict observance of the principle that in determining all such questions of sovereignty *the interests of the populations concerned must have equal weight with the equitable claims of the government whose title is to be determined*' (emphasis added). While Wilson accepted the reality of colonialism, therefore, he insisted that European interests could not be paramount over those of colonial peoples.

America and colonialism: an ambiguous relationship

It would be wrong to take Wilson's high moral tone as representative of all US opinion. In reality, the American relationship with colonialism was complex and ambivalent. The United States had itself taken part in the new imperial acquisitiveness at the end of the previous century. Although not amassing a colonial empire on anything like the scale of Britain, France or Germany, the United States took possession of various territories after the Spanish-American war of 1898. By the Treaty of Paris which ended the war, the Philippines in south-east Asia and the Pacific island of Guam passed to the USA. In the Caribbean, Cuba came under American military occupation and Puerto Rico was annexed (bringing a final end to four centuries of Spanish colonialism in the Americas which had begun with the first landing of Christopher Columbus). During the same period Congress resolved a long-standing and complex relationship with Britain and France over the nominally independent territory of Hawaii by simply voting to annex it.

It was possible of course to present this new imperial status as a paradoxical and unintended consequence of an anti-colonial war against Spain and righteous exasperation with the imperial games of Britain and France. Yet, there were also influential voices in the United States who found the idea of an American empire quite attractive. America, they argued, had a God-given 'manifest destiny' to expand in the Pacific. The objective was not, of course,

America, they argued, had a God-given manifest destiny to expand in the Pacific.

vulgar acquisition but a New World version of the civilizing mission – which needless to say would be more progressive and democratically rooted than any European model.

The expression 'manifest destiny' had been coined originally in the 1840s, not as a rationalization of tropical imperialism but to justify the process of expansion which was then pushing the American frontier westwards from Atlantic to Pacific. In this original sense the manifest destiny of the United States was to take control of former Spanish territories in Texas, California and New Mexico. However, by the end of the century the Pacific coastline was no longer regarded as the final and natural barrier to the fulfilment of this destiny. Instead, the ocean itself provided the next phase of expansion.

By the last years of the nineteenth century the sides in the debate between those advocating this colonizing role and their anti-imperialist counterparts reflected approximately the positions of the two main political parties in the United States. The Republicans, most colourfully represented by future President Theodore Roosevelt who had himself fought the Spanish in Cuba, urged expansion. The Democrats remained wary of anything that offended the fundamental distaste for imperialism that was rooted in America's political culture. The latter position was personified at the end of the First World War by Woodrow Wilson.

Neither party, it should be said, had any moral qualms or practical doubts about the expansion of the continental frontier and the huge act of internal colonialism this involved. The dispossession of North America's native population and the destruction of its cultures were simply not recognized as part of the debate. Overland expansion in the original sense of 'manifest destiny', the advance of the internal frontier, was seen universally as a cause for national celebration. Continental America remained in this sense an ever-spreading colony of settlement, and a wholly unapologetic one.

The League of Nations and the mandate system

With the United States dominance unchallengeable at the Versailles peace conference in 1919, Wilson was able to impose his view of the post-war world on the other allies. Neither Britain nor France was in a position to argue him down, and were both probably incapable of speaking with a united voice on the range of challenges facing the victorious allies in any case.

The most tangible expression of the Wilsonian world view was the new League of Nations. The last of the Fourteen Points had called for the creation of a 'general association of nations ... formed under specific covenants for the purpose of affording mutual guarantees of political independence and territorial integrity to great and small states alike'. The ultimate purpose of this was to supplant national defence arrangements with a global system of collective security. This would remove the 'security dilemmas', whether expressed in arms races or pre-emptive colonial acquisitions, which had been such a dangerous feature of the pre-war international system. The basic structures of the League – its executive Council, its quasi-parliamentary Assembly and its permanent civil service – inevitably drew comparisons with those of a national government. The comparison was strengthened by the fact that the League also had a 'constitution'. The Covenant laid down the objectives and powers of the organization across a wide spectrum of international security and political issues, including the fate of the colonies removed from those who had lost the war.

The section of the Covenant dealing with colonialism was in a very real sense revolutionary. The essence of the new 'mandate' system was that, in a break with immemorial historical practice, the imperial possessions of the defeated should not simply pass as spoils of war to the victors. Instead, their administration was to become the *responsibility* of suitable powers until such time as they were ready for independent statehood. A mandate was designed to be an intermediate stage on the way to the same self-determination that had been granted to the former territor-ies of the defeated empires in central and eastern Europe. This approach reflected Wilson's moral world view, but the idea had been taken up by interested parties in Europe as well. The British Labour Party was an enthusiastic advocate of the system as the most practical and 'anti-colonialist' solution to an unavoidable reality. The Foreign Office in London did not oppose the approach as it offered a clear legal framework within which potentially tricky post-war adjustments could be made.

Article 22 of the League Covenant dealt with the colonial aftermath of the war with a degree of detail unusual elsewhere in the document. It pronounced that:

To those colonies and territories which as a consequence of the late war have ceased to be under the sovereignty of the states which formerly governed them and which are inhabited by peoples not yet able to stand by themselves under the strenuous conditions of the modern world, there should be applied the principle that the well-being and development of such peoples form a sacred trust of civilization and that securities for the performance of this trust should be embodied in this Covenant.

The best method of giving practical effect to this principle is that the tutelage of such peoples should be entrusted to advanced nations who by reason of their resources, their experience or their geographical position can best undertake this responsibility, and who are willing to accept it, and that this tutelage should be exercised by them as Mandatories on behalf of the League.

These mandatories were to submit annual reports on each of the territories for which they had responsibility to a Permanent Mandates Commission. The members of the Commission were prominent private individuals, appointed by the League Council rather than nominated by their own countries. In fact, most members were not even citizens of mandatory states. This allowed the Commission to perform a highly political function without the complication of inter-state politics. The International Labour Office, one of the League's new specialized agencies, was to be prominently represented on the Commission. This reflected concerns that had been widespread internationally since the beginning of the century over colonial labour practices. The sins of Belgian and Portuguese Africa in particular had been condemned in Europe and the United States before the war and were not to be tolerated on the League's watch.

The sins of Belgian and Portuguese Africa in particular had been condemned in Europe and the United States before the war and were not to be tolerated on the League's watch.

The system was designed to be sensitive to the cultural and political setting of different mandated territories. As the Covenant put it: 'the character of the mandate must differ according to the stage of the development of the people, the geographical situation of the territory, its economic conditions, and other similar circumstances'. There were to be three classes of mandate.

The first of these, the 'A' mandates, was applied to the Arab lands from which Turkey had been expelled at the end of the war. These territories were judged to be close to the conditions necessary for successful independence. The role of the mandatory power here was merely to provide 'administrative advice and assistance ... until such time as they are able to stand alone'. Britain and France were the two countries to which these Middle Eastern territories were mandated. It proved a considerable responsibility, even a burden, for both of them. During the war Arab nationalism had been deliberately encouraged, particularly by Britain (most romantically in the person of Lawrence of Arabia) as a weapon against Turkey. Expectations of immediate independence in the region after the defeat of the Ottoman empire were therefore high. One of the most difficult mandates was Iraq, where three largely separate regions and different Muslim sects were brought together to form an uneasy administrative unit. This became Britain's responsibility and in the 1920s it proved, as it would many years later, to be a much greater challenge for the forces of occupation than originally anticipated. Britain was also the mandatory for Transjordan (modern-day Jordan). Perhaps the most poisoned of the Arab chalices passed to the British, however, was Palestine. The location of the new state of Israel in 1948, it would confront Britain with one of its most difficult overseas challenges in the immediate post Second World War years. France was made responsible for Syria and, the most westernized and multi-ethnic of the Arab territories, Lebanon. Both of these claimed their independence while France was under German occupation during the Second World War and effectively found their own way to statehood at that time.

The 'B' mandates related to the former German colonies of sub-Saharan Africa. These were places which were, in the words of the Covenant,

at such a stage that the Mandatory must be responsible for the admin-istration of the territory under conditions which will guarantee freedom of conscience and religion, subject only to the maintenance of public order and morals, the prohibition of abuses such as the slave trade, the arms traffic, and the liquor traffic . . .

Britain became responsible for German East Africa (Tanganyika) which had borders with the British possessions of Kenya in the north and Northern Rhodesia in the south. Joined in something of a forced and not entirely happy marriage with the island of Zanzibar, Tanganyika became the independent state of Tanzania in 1964. Britain and France together took responsibility for Togoland and the Cameroons, which adjoined their own West African possessions. On the same principle of territorial contiguity, the colonies of Ruanda and Urundi (modern-day Rwanda and Burundi), which neighboured the Congo in the Great Lakes region of central Africa, were placed under Belgian mandate. Here, Belgium maintained Germany's policy of divide and rule between the two main ethnic groups – the Hutus and the Tutsis – which in the 1990s would contribute to some of the most murderous acts in a century already well marked by genocide.

The final group, the 'C' mandates, were special cases that, in apparent contradiction of the basic principle of the mandate system, 'were best administered under the laws of the

Mandatory as integral portions of its territory'. The Covenant presented them as such on the grounds of their small size, sparse population or remoteness. However, in at least one case, that of German South West Africa, the real reason for its special position was the insistence of the mandatory, South Africa, that it should effectively become an extension of the national territory. This situation would lead to protracted violence and troubled international involvement at the end of the century. After the Second World War Apartheid South Africa tried first to prevent and then delay the independence of the new state of Namibia, creating a slow-burning crisis that was only resolved through superpower diplomacy and UN peacekeeping.

Interestingly, all but one of the 'C' mandatories had themselves been colonies of settlement within the British Empire. Australia became responsible for the vast and still largely unexplored territory of German New Guinea. This adjoined Australia's existing protectorate of Papua. Australia was also mandatory for the tiny island of Nauru. New Zealand was to be responsible for Western Samoa. (The adjoining islands comprised American Samoa, another fragment of America's 'manifest destiny' in the Pacific that had been annexed by the United States at the end of the nineteenth century.) The other 'C' mandatory was Japan, which became responsible for three small former German territories in Micronesia that would later mark the geographical limit of Japanese expansion during the Second World War.

This new approach to colonial relations was certainly novel and more or less admirable, but much of the general optimism around the League's attempt to build a new world order soon evaporated. The decade of the 1920s was largely free of high international tensions, but this was more a result of post-war exhaustion than any new security mechanisms. By the early 1930s pressures had built once again between states determined to maintain the territorial and political status quo and others determined to disrupt it. Woodrow Wilson's vision of a new type of international system had not been realized – and his commitment to liberal interventionism had not been shared by the US Congress, which had refused to ratify American membership of the League.

Despite the larger failure of the League project, however, the colonial mandate system endured and was taken over by the United Nations in 1945 as a fully functioning mechanism. The philosophical underpinnings of the mandate approach influenced the wider debate about colonialism between the wars. The idea of post-war colonial adjustment, involving a 'sacred trust' rather than a simple transfer of assets, affected thinking about the final destination of colonial rule in both the European imperial countries and in the colonies themselves. One can of course argue that this 'tutelage' was no more than an elaboration on the 'civilizing mission' which every colonialist state claimed to be engaged in anyway. But the League institutionalized and legitimized a particular form of 'progressive' colonialism and gave it a certain legitimacy in international law. In short, the League challenged the pieties and hypocrisies of national colonial thinking and encouraged the development of a new international ethic.

THE INTERWAR YEARS: COLONIALISM IN QUESTION

The colonialism of the Axis powers

With the reversion to international instability in the 1930s a new phase of colonialism began.

With the reversion to international instability in the 1930s a new phase of colonialism began. Nazi Germany's expansionism – its pursuit of *Lebensraum* ('living space') in central and eastern Europe – was in some respects an attempt to revive the continental imperialism that had been laid to rest at Versailles in 1919. The Nazis did not appear to have any strong interest in reviving the tropical empire that had been stripped from Germany and parcelled out as mandates after the First World War however. The reconfiguration of Europe was ambition enough in the meantime, though a triumphant Third Reich would obviously take control of the colonial empires of those it had defeated. Early in the war the Nazis thought of using the French colony of Madagascar as one possible solution to their central obsession, the 'Jewish problem'. The forced mass resettlement of European Jews there was considered for a time, but abandoned. The predicted collapse of Britain early in the war did not happen, denying Germany control of the seas. Genocide became the preferred option.

Germany's allies were more enthusiastic about long-range colonialism. The aggressive, territorially greedy regimes in Italy and Japan saw imperial expansion as a fundamental qualification for the world power status they craved. Whatever the moral and practical achievements of the mandate system, the League of Nations failed dismally to resist this. It did not provide the 'mutual guarantees of political independence and territorial

integrity to great and small states alike' that Wilson had prom-
ised in his Fourteen Points. On the contrary, the League proved
utterly supine when these principles were challenged in Africa
and Asia.

Italy had been one of the lesser players in the imperial game of
the previous century. Then, like Germany, it had only recently
been unified as a single state and its political class saw an overseas empire as an imprimatur of its status as a major European
power. However, its efforts to acquire one met with very mixed
success. A relative latecomer to the scramble for Africa, Italy
found its options were limited. In the late 1880s and early 1890s
it managed to acquire territory in the inhospitable and unproductive north-east of the continent, in the Horn of Africa. The larger
part of modern-day Somalia was seized at this time, along with
Eritrea further to the north on the Red Sea coast. These beginnings spurred Italy's ambitions, but its possibilities were limited.
Britain and France already had a presence in north-east Africa and
were hardly going to be ejected by a colonial parvenu like Italy.

The government in Rome therefore decided to annex the one
part of the region where direct conflict with other colonizers was
not an issue: the independent African kingdom of Abyssinia
(modern-day Ethiopia). The war launched by Italy against
Abyssinia in pursuit of this in 1895–96 was disastrous for its
emerging self-image as a major European player. The fiercely
independent Abyssinians brought Italy's imperial ambitions to a
humiliating end at the Battle of Adowa in 1896. Defeat at the
hands of a supposedly uncivilized, lesser race that it had marked
down to become colonial subjects was an unprecedented humiliation for a European country. It was not something that Italy's
insecure national sense of self would easily absorb. Later, Italy

did manage to extend its overseas empire when it ejected an already weak Ottoman presence from modern-day Libya and tried to develop it as a colony of settlement. The colonial model here seemed to be that of France in Algeria, where a close colonial relationship had been established across the relatively small sea distance of the Mediterranean. East Africa and the defeat at Adowa still rankled, however, and when the Fascists came to power in Rome it could be predicted that they would attempt to avenge the slight to national honour.

Territorial aggrandizement was an intrinsic component of the Fascist ideology. Relatively densely populated and without any great natural resources, Italy naturally looked outwards. It was already at the beginning of the twentieth century a major source of migrants to North America, for example. Fascism, however, preferred to expand national territory rather than export national population. Around the near European horizon the obstacles to territorial expansion were intimidating. Italian Fascism had nothing comparable to the military resources of German Nazism. When the Second World War began, Italy occupied Albania and parts of Yugoslavia and Greece, but this was a strategic rather than a colonial project. The major imperial focus remained Africa in the febrile ambition of the Italian dictator Benito Mussolini. An Italian East African empire, enlarged to absorb Abyssinia, could become a vast colony of settlement. It would provide an 'Italian' rather than a foreign destination for legions of impoverished peasants from the south of Italy. It would also be a tangible Fascist achievement, an indelible mark of Italian imperial greatness. Accordingly, in 1935 Italy launched a new war against Abyssinia from its colony of Eritrea. This time air-power and armoured vehicles guaranteed Italy's victory.

The fate of Abyssinia and the world's failure to do anything to rescue it proved to be a milestone on the League of Nations' road to moral and diplomatic irrelevance. Britain and France, the major powers on the League Council, played the issue by the rules of nineteenth-century European realpolitik. The principles of the new collective security that the League was supposed to embody simply did not figure. Statements of protest were made and inadequate economic sanctions agreed. The reality, though, was that neither Britain nor France saw any immediate national interest in making an enemy of Italy, particularly over an issue that was, after all, merely 'colonial'. The newsreel image of the Abyssinian monarch, Haile Selassie, addressing the League in a dignified but unavailing attempt to persuade it to act on its responsibilities became a symbol of the moral degradation of the organization.

Japan had occupied an odd position in the diplomacy of the late nineteenth and early twentieth centuries when Europe's colonizing energies were at their height.

In Asia too colonialism was to be an important element in the war. Japan had occupied an odd position in the diplomacy of the late nineteenth and early twentieth centuries when Europe's colonizing energies were at their height. It stood apart from its Asian neighbours, having modernized its economy and already become something of an industrial powerhouse in the second half of the nineteenth century. While other nominally independent Asian states like China and Thailand were effectively semi-colonies at this time, Japan took command of its own economic and political destiny. In 1902 it signed a naval treaty with Britain, the first non-European country to establish such a relationship. Three years later it humbled Russia in a land and sea war for primacy in north Asia. In the years before 1914 Japan had been keen to annex neighbouring territory to expand its limited national resource base. The island of Formosa (Taiwan) was occupied in 1895 and, more ambitiously, the Korean peninsula was seized in 1910. Away from the sight and interests of the major powers, these acts of colonization were largely ignored by the wider world.

Like Italy, Japan had fought on the winning side in the First World War and, like Italy too, had a radical militarist regime which saw territorial expansion as a marker of its importance in the international system. Its annexations of territory from its enfeebled neighbour China in the 1930s had, along with Italy's rape of Abyssinia, exposed the hollowness of the League's pretensions to collective security. Here too, the European powers saw no benefit to their interests in confronting a powerful state merely doing what colonialists do in the colonial world.

Where Japan's colonialism departed from that of Italy was in its restriction to its 'home' Asia-Pacific region. This continental vista eventually brought Japan into conflict with the established colonial empires of Europe and the United States. For a time, this allowed Japan to present its expansionism as a kind of anti-colonial liberation war rather than what it was, brutal colonization. In the early 1940s the Japanese swept down through the Malayan peninsula to Singapore, across the Indonesian archipelago, through the Philippines and Indo-China to the very borders of British India. Japanese power also stretched into the Pacific, threatening northern Australia from New Guinea. One by one, Britain, France, the Netherlands, the

United States and Australia had been knocked from their positions of colonial dominance. As European power collapsed in this way before the Asian onslaught, it was possible to see Japan's expansion as Asia's payback for the humiliation of European colonialism and as an exercise in pan-Asian nationalism.

The reality was quite different. Japan's drive to create a so-called 'greater Asian co-prosperity sphere' was simply a vast imperial project. It was, moreover, one characterized by a level of racial contempt at least as great as that of any European colonialist. And it was wholly unqualified by even the rhetoric of 'tutelage' which had been central to the European colonial discourse since the establishment of the League of Nations. The territories in which European power was extinguished did not become independent entities, but found themselves under a new and more brutal form of colonial bondage. Thailand and the occupied parts of China ceased to be semi-colonies of the west and became actual colonies of Japan.

The end of the war saw these Italian and Japanese projects dismantled just as the end of the previous one had brought the dissolution of the German and Turkish colonial empires. In Africa, Abyssinia was restored to independence following a counter invasion from the Sudan by British and local forces. Italy was further punished after the war when, no doubt driven in part by guilt for their inactivity in 1935, the allies agreed that Eritrea should become in effect a province of Ethiopia (as Abyssinia was now more commonly known). In a tragic and bloody irony, the Eritreans themselves saw this as merely a further act of colonization – a situation resolved only after a long and destructive liberation war and Eritrea's final independence in 1993. Libya,

scene of heavy desert fighting during the war, became independent in 1952 after a period of United Nations supervision.
Italian Somaliland joined with its British counterpart to become
independent Somalia in 1960. In Asia, meantime, Japan had been
forced back behind its pre-war borders. Korea and Formosa
became, in their different complex ways, independent entities – in
both cases creating new difficulties for post-war international
relations.

Despite these readjustments there could be no return to the
imperial status quo ante in Asia. Japanese expansionism had a
double-headed effect on the European colonial possessions in
Asia. For one thing, the early stages of the war had exposed the
myth of European invulnerability. No matter how atrocious
Japanese occupation may have been, no matter how far removed
it was from any real act of liberation, the inescapable fact was
that an Asian power had humiliated the European masters. But,
secondly, the Japanese occupation of Asian lands had provoked a
new spirit of nationalism in them. Driven initially by anti-
Japanese sentiment, this national resistance merged with the
sense of enablement against European colonialism that Japan
itself had encouraged. Throughout the region nationalist politicians and guerrilla fighters turned their wrath on the old
masters, having contributed to the defeat of their more recent
ones. Just as the end of the First World War brought a fundamental change in the way colonialism was perceived in the wider
world, after the Second World War the pressure for its total
eradication would become irresistible.

Recommended reading

The most exhaustive account of the League and the mandate system remains a book first published in 1952 by its former deputy secretary-general, Francis (F.P.) Walters – *A History of the League of Nations* (Oxford: Oxford University Press, 1969). There has been a dearth of material published on the League in recent years. F.S. Northedge's *The League of Nations: Its Life and Times, 1920–1946* (Leicester: Leicester University Press, 1985) is still useful, though stronger on general security issues than on colonialism.

At least as far as colonial issues are concerned, the situation has been retrieved recently by Michael Callahan's two-volume study of the mandate system in Africa – *Mandates and Empire: The League of Nations and Africa, 1914–1931* and *A Sacred Trust: The League of Nations and Africa, 1929–1946* (Brighton: Sussex Academic Press, 1999 and 2004).

Beyond Africa, D.K. Fieldhouse's *Western Imperialism in the Middle East, 1914–1958* (London: Oxford University Press, 2006) deals with a critical period in the colonial history of the Arab lands. Japan's colonization of large parts of Asia in the 1930s and early 1940s is dealt with by W.G. Beasley in *Japanese Imperialism, 1894–1945* (London: Oxford University Press, 1991).

British colonialism in the interwar years is covered exhaustively in *The Twentieth Century* (London: Oxford University Press, 1999), volume IV of the *Oxford History of the British Empire*, which is edited by Andrew Porter.

CHAPTER 4

European 'cultures' of colonial rule

AFTER THE END of the Second World War four large tropical empires remained: those of Belgium, Britain, France and Portugal. Germany and Italy had been stripped of their colonies after the First and Second World Wars respectively. Spain, moribund and inward-looking under the reactionary rule of General Franco, held on to fragments in North and West Africa but had long ceased to be a significant colonial force. The United States, never wholly comfortable in the role of colonial master, withdrew from the Philippines in 1946. Holland was impoverished and enfeebled after the war and incapable of re-establishing itself in Asia in the face of radical Indonesian nationalism.

The Belgian empire in Africa, though vast in territorial terms, was confined to the Congo–Great Lakes region. Belgium's colonialism had always been pragmatic. It began with the creation of a personal economic fiefdom by King Léopold II in the Congo, the hideously misnamed 'Congo Free State' (which not by accident was the setting of Joseph Conrad's 1902 grim novella *The*

Heart of Darkness). In 1908 the Congo was taken over by the Belgian state amidst international scandal over the avarice and violence with which Léopold pillaged its wealth. Rwanda and Burundi came unsought as mandates after Germany's defeat in 1918. In contrast to the other three major post-1945 imperial powers, Belgium was something of an accidental colonialist, and its politicians and intellectuals spent little energy on contemplating the meaning and purpose of the colonial vocation.

In contrast, the remaining three empires – British, French and Portuguese – did engage to varying degrees in philosophical rationalizations for their colonial policies and practices. In this they occupied different points on a broad spectrum of colonial 'theology'. At one end lay Britain's generally expedient approach to its colonial role. By the end of the Second World War the British were already realistic about the limited future of empire. France, on the other hand, was more damaged

> *By the end of the Second World War the British were already realistic about the limited future of empire.*

physically and spiritually than Britain in 1945 and perhaps because rather than in spite of this it seemed less able to contemplate the end of its imperial status. Culturally, France's psychological line of retreat was more difficult than that of Britain. French colonialism had a much more elaborate philosophical rationale than the British variety, a reflection perhaps of two quite different intellectual traditions. The French penchant for the abstractions of theory was at odds with British empiricism. Portugal lay further still along the spectrum of abstraction, beyond France. By far the weakest of the European colonial powers in 1945 despite its not having participated in the war,

Portugal displayed an approach to empire that was both complex and monolithic. Its view was shaped by the long experience of its three successive empires in Asia, Brazil and Africa respectively. In contrast to Britain, and to a greater extent even than France, Portugal regarded its colonial empire as a central component of national self-esteem. Economically and socially underdeveloped itself, Portugal leant on its 'single and indivisible' empire as a political and psychological prop.

Britain: variety and pragmatism

The history of British colonialism saw none of the sharp discontinuities of either its French or Portuguese counterparts. The British Empire at its height was a product of the incremental accumulation of a wide range of different types of colonial possession. It was not the result of a sequence of sudden gain, loss and reacquisition. Even putting aside its cultural preference for expedient empiricism, a 'one-size-fits-all' approach to the imperial role like that adopted by Portugal (and to some extent by France as well) would have been all but impossible. Canada and Australia were hardly comparable to India, let alone Nigeria or the Solomon Islands. Unguided by any all-inclusive philosophy, British colonial practice varied widely. So far as there was a unifying strand to British imperial administration, it was the paradoxical one of 'indirect rule', a policy of co-opting local rulers and, with due adjustments, local forms of rule.

India provides the most obvious example of this. In parts of the British Raj, local maharajas retained considerable power and even enjoyed the outward symbols of obeisance from the local European agents of the empire. In this way an entire stratum of the traditional ruling class in India was drawn into the colonial project. In return for a British guarantee of their continued privileged position, they 'delivered' their domains to the empire. Over time these rulers and their children would be educated in the elite schools and universities of the imperial 'motherland' and would often become simulacrums of the 'typical' English gentleman. Arguably, this was a more effective if less direct means of tying the colony to the culture of the motherland than to attempt its forced absorption. Radical critics certainly saw it as a key device in easing the transition from colonial control to neocolonial exploitation after formal independence.

Similar systems to the Indian one were put in place by British administrators elsewhere in Asia, most notably in Malaya. The approach also extended, though less consistently, to some parts of Africa as well, particularly West Africa. It is here that we meet perhaps as close to a philosopher-practitioner of British colonialism as the empire produced: Frederick (in later life, Lord) Lugard. There were, of course, other British voices to be heard, such as that of Rudyard Kipling with his paternalistic view of the white man's burden. There were also turn-of-the-century politicians like the liberal imperialist Joseph Chamberlain and administrators like Alfred Milner in southern Africa who had distinctive views on the importance, economic and political, of colonialism to the motherland. And, of course, there were also those like Cecil Rhodes (of 'Rhodesia') who had strong views about the importance of colonialism to themselves. Lugard, however, provides us with a rounded, closely considered sense of British colonialism. It was a view grounded in the successive roles of an explorer, soldier, administrator and, finally, international elder statesman. It was distilled from the accumulated experience of a lifetime's engagement with colonialism stretching from the 1880s until the 1940s.

Over his life Lugard witnessed and shaped the colonial process from India to the Nile and across sub-Saharan Africa. He had been involved in the confrontation with the French over spheres of control in north-west Africa that led to the Fashoda crisis in 1898. At a later stage in his career he served for five years as governor of Hong Kong. But he is most closely associated in the history of British colonial policy and practice with Nigeria, where he spent two lengthy terms in charge of the colonial government from 1900 until the end of the First World War. His most celebrated achievement there was the unification of the Muslim north and the Animist/Christian south into a single colony. 'Celebrated', that is to say, by British colonial interests. It is less clear whether this enforced unification was welcomed by Nigerians, who have periodically found themselves engulfed in inter-regional conflict. The dreadful Biafran war of secession in the late 1960s was only the most destructive of these. A unified Nigeria, however, was in Britain's larger imperial interests in West Africa – and Lugard delivered it. During his time there, he managed to mitigate some of these regionalist tensions through a carefully calibrated policy of indirect rule. Local chiefs and religious leaders were left to get on with the job of governing with the degree of British oversight adjusted to local circumstances. In general, British intervention was limited to the prevention of slave trading and the infliction of excessive

In general, British intervention was limited to the prevention of slave trading and the infliction of excessive judicial punishments

judicial punishments – and, of course, the discouragement of any tendency to question the fundamentals of the colonial relationship.

Frederick (Lord) Lugard (1858–1945)

Lugard was born to missionary parents in India. He became a professional soldier after a conventional English public school education and achieved rapid promotion in the swirl of British imperial campaigns during the 1880s and 1890s. His service ranged across the globe, from India to east and central Africa and on to Hong Kong (where he served as governor). He had an extremely colourful and romantic early life, involving tragic love affairs, buccaneering anti-slavery actions and confrontations with rival imperial armies. Lugard has been most closely associated with West Africa, and in particular Nigeria. Here he was instrumental in creating a unified colony, bringing together the Christian and Animist south with the Muslim north in uneasy partnership. His most enduring contribution to British imperial policy, however, lay in his innovative approach to colonial administration. He was an advocate and practitioner of 'indirect rule'. This in principle enabled a small corps of British officials to manage vast areas through 'light touch' supervision of traditional local rulers. Lugard described this approach in his celebrated book *The Dual Mandate in British Tropical Africa*. With the establishment of the League of Nations after the First World War he became a highly respected member of the Mandates Commission, which was responsible for the oversight of the colonies taken from the defeated powers. He was ennobled in 1928 and as a member of the House of Lords was prominent in parliamentary debates on colonial issues until late in life.

This was an approach to colonization which, in West Africa as in India, served multiple interests. It minimized anti-colonial resentment by sustaining traditional forms of rule. It maintained traditional power structures under conditions of 'tutelage' which would ease the move to self-determination and independence when and if it came. But, perhaps most persuasively for the hard-headed men of the Colonial Office, it provided colonial administration on the cheap. In effect, the colonized bore the cost of their colonization. Lugard's own rationalization for the policy had nothing to do with administrative parsimony. His views on the interrelated concepts of indirect rule and colonial tutelage were laid out at length and in detail in his famous account, *The Dual Mandate in British Tropical Africa*, published in 1922. Here, he developed the idea of colonialism as a symbiotic encounter between colonized and colonizer. Both could – and should – benefit in different ways from the relationship if it was properly conducted. The colonizer gained through new opportunities for trade and commerce. The colonized meanwhile benefited from the arrival of new manufactured goods and the blessings of externally supervised order. It was a pragmatic arrangement, in other words, but one with potentially progressive outcomes.

Colonial rule was in the interests of the colonized because, as he put it in *The Dual Mandate*, the 'subject races of Africa are not yet able to stand alone, and . . . it would not conduce to the happiness of the vast bulk of the people' if they tried to do so. However, that was not to say that the relationship would be a permanent one. Indirect rule was a flexible and dynamic process which would naturally tend to move towards ever-greater levels of local autonomy and, eventually, independent statehood. It was not an approach that could be applied in a blanket fashion, of course. 'Obviously the extent to which native races are capable of controlling their own affairs must vary in proportion to their degree of development and progress in social organization, but this is a question of adaptation not of principle'. The destination was a metropolitan model of statehood: 'the ideal of self-government can only be realized by the methods of evolution which have produced the democracies of Europe and America' (*The Dual Mandate in British Tropical Africa* [1922], p. 195). But it was a destination.

> *Lugard was often at odds with his masters in London, who were wary of his colourful past and lone-wolf ways.*

Lugard was often at odds with his masters in London, who were wary of his colourful past and lone-wolf ways. He was also notoriously unwilling to delegate to more junior officials on the ground. It was something of a paradox that, while he was committed to the diffusion of power among traditional rulers, he was much less ready to entrust it to his own staff. None of this, however, prevented him developing a devoted following among younger colonial policy makers and local officers in the years before the First World War.

After the war his burgeoning reputation as Britain's pre-eminent thinker on colonialism was confirmed by the publication of *The Dual Mandate*. With the establishment of the League of Nations, Lugard became an obvious choice for appointment to the Mandates Commission. There, his contribution to the development of the basic idea of colonialism as 'tutelage' was widely recognized. As the deputy secretary-general of the League, Francis Walters, later wrote, the 'conception of a sacred trust was not new (but) no one had done so much to teach it and to (practise) it as the man who was for many years the greatest figure in the Mandates Commission'

(F.P. Walters, *A History of the League of Nations* [1952], pp. 172–3).

The pragmatism in which the idea of indirect rule and colonial tutelage were embedded represented flexibility in a sense. But in some respects it was a static, even conservative approach to colonial development. It tended to solidify traditional forms of authority that might in the normal (non-colonial) course of events have been supplanted by more forward-looking institutions. In other words, the supposedly 'progressive' colonial incursion could perpetuate historical inefficiencies and injustices. The bloody post-colonial history of Kashmir, for example, a major source of conflict between India and Pakistan since their independence, would probably have been quite different if it had not been subject to indirect rule within the empire. At the time of independence in 1947, predominantly Muslim Kashmir was ruled by a Hindu maharaja whose favoured position with the British allowed him to take the territory into India rather than Pakistan. The consequence has been continuous ethnic and international conflict on one of the world's most sensitive borders.

Moreover, indirect rule through traditional power structures with a parallel preparation for self-determination may have been options in colonies without large European populations. It was a less viable option in colonies of settlement where traditional local structures could conflict with white power. British self-congratulation over the supposed down-to-earth practicality of its approach to colonialism is not entirely justified, in such circumstances. But did the more 'uni-formal' continental approach to the colonial project fare any better in practice?

France: *'assimilation'* and *'association'*

Where the British approach to colonial administration was shaped by variations in the colonial setting, the French one was strongly centralized. Where Britain regarded its empire as fundamentally 'apart' from the metropolis (however strong the bonds of culture and sentiment), France took a much more 'integrative' view. Its colonies were *France outre-mer* ('overseas France'). Although its tropical territories might not be physically contiguous with the metropolis, they were politically, even spiritually, extensions of European France. It was not the purpose of French colonialism to rule for a set period through local structures until such time as 'barbarism' had been supplanted by 'law and order', (as Lugard's writings implied) and then depart. The very *idea* of France would be implanted perman-ently in its colonies and the prospect of their having a long-term future that was not 'French' was rarely considered.

The sources of this mindset lie in great part in French Enlightenment thinking, along with a marked and long-standing preference in French political culture for administrative centralism. At the end of the eighteenth century France, by its own estimation, provided the light and the way for the rest of the world. The French revolutionaries were convinced that their humanist vision was universally applicable – and therefore exportable – to all parts of the world. Even if France's neighbours in Europe were so misguided as to reject this gift, later generations of French leaders reasoned that it was still a valid currency for the rest of the world. For France, therefore, the *mission civilisatrice* was more specific than the civilizing missions pursued by Britain and the United States. It had to do with the exportation of uniquely French attitudes rather than vaguely defined 'progressive' ones. The expression used for this was *rayonnement* – an illumination of the way. The light provided, of course, would be refracted through the prism of French culture and intellectual traditions.

At the day-to-day political level the idea of colonial integration was in many respects simply an extension of the high degree of centralization in metropolitan France. This had been a feature of French domestic administration since the time of Napoleon (and remains so). By the twentieth century, for example, it was observed that at any point in a given day one could look at one's watch and know what every French child of a particular age was learning in school at that precise moment. For a considerable period, adjusted for time-zones, this pedagogic synchronicity applied far beyond the shores of European France itself.

> *By the twentieth century, for example, it was observed that at any point in a given day one could look at one's watch and know what every French child of a particular age was learning in school at that precise moment.*

It may be, too, that France's geographical position encouraged an integrative philosophy of colonialism. France is an Atlantic power and saw itself as part of the 'advanced' – that is to say northern – European community of nations in the nineteenth century. But it is also a Mediterranean country whose southern waters look directly across to North Africa. The jewels of its colonial crown, most particularly Algeria, may not have been territorially contiguous with metropolitan France, but they had a much closer physical proximity than, say, that between India and Britain. Even at the most practical level, movement between French metropolis and North African colony was quick, physically easy and relatively economic long before the arrival of air travel. And, from Algeria across the Sahara and then onwards west and south, a large part of *France outre-mer* indeed *was* geographically contiguous.

As usual with strong assertions of cultural identity, neurosis lurked just below the surface of the French position. France's imperial project in the nineteenth and twentieth centuries has to be seen (much more than that of Britain) as an extension of European insecurities. Defeat in 1815 led to colonial adventure in Algeria in the 1830s. Humiliation at the hands of Prussia in 1873 was a preliminary to France's headlong plunge into the scramble for West and Equatorial Africa. Colonial expansion provided the stamp of great power status for France (just as it did for the even more insecure Italy). The millions of subject people acquired as a result, provided a blank sheet of humanity on which the superiority of French intellectual and political culture could be inscribed.

The colonial policy that grew from this psychological loam was that of *assimilation*. The political roots of *assimilation* were to be found in the crucible of the French Revolution. Quite admirably taking the principles of human liberty, equality and fraternity to their logical conclusion, the revolutionaries of the 1790s extended full political rights to the peoples of the French colonial possessions of the time. Local representation in the French national legislature and manhood franchise were granted to at least the settled populations of the tropical possessions. A Frenchman, regardless of race or skin colour, was a Frenchman and was therefore bestowed with the natural rights of all Frenchmen. In this way, France was transformed into an *idea* rather than a mere colonial metropolis. As the bounds of the empire expanded – to North Africa in the first half of the nineteenth century and then south of the Sahara and to south-east Asia – the world's tally of Frenchmen expanded with them.

The flaw in this apparently commendable and progressive approach to colonial rule, however, was that it assumed the colonized people *were* French and that their indigenous cultures were inferior to that of the European metropolis. Although inherently non-racist in its basic suppositions about human potential, it was profoundly racist at the cultural level. This was a theme explored by the great psychoanalyst of colonialism, Frantz Fanon. Born in French Martinique in 1925, Fanon became committed to the struggle for Algerian independence in the 1960s. His seminal work was *Black Skin, White Masks*, published in 1952. Here, he anatomized the psychological and cultural damage inflicted on the colonized by a colonial philosophy which on the one hand celebrated the universality of a European identity (the 'white mask') while on the other despising the prior identity of the subject peoples.

Frantz Fanon (1925–1961)

Born in Martinique in the French Caribbean, Fanon was by profession a psychiatrist. He completed his studies at the University of Lyon after service in the French army during the Second World War. In this professional capacity he was concerned with the societal bases of mental disorder, an interest that inspired much of his writings on the psychology of colonialism. His first major book, *Black Skin, White Masks* (1952), explored from a personal perspective the alienating impact of colonialism on the psyche of the 'native' subject. In the early 1950s his clinical work took him to Algeria where he became involved in the liberation struggle against French rule and he soon rose to prominence in the National Liberation Front (FNL), the dominant anti-colonial movement at war with France. In 1961 he published another celebrated work, the *Wretched of the Earth*, a call to colonized people to seize control of their situation, if necessary through the use of revolutionary force. His role in the FNL along with the uncompromising style of his writings has led some to caricature him as a ruthless apostle of violence. In reality, his perspective, although unbendingly anti-colonialist, was a complex and nuanced one.

In practice, *assimilation* was a philosophy often more honoured in the breach than in the observance. In periods of conservative rule in France (that is, for much of the nineteenth and twentieth centuries), the citizenship rights of the colonized were usually ignored. Achieving the status of assimilated citizen in the first place became subject to all sorts of economic and educational barriers that were set unrealistically high. The rigid centralization that was an essential part of the assimilation policy did not vary, however, and French rule usually loomed heavily and brutally over the colonies.

By the end of the Second World War the policy of assimilation had more or less unravelled. France, in much the same way as it had after 1815 and 1873, looked to the colonies to soften harsh European realities. In other words, France was determined to maintain its empire as a comfort blanket against its degraded position in its own continent. In contrast to Britain, where powerful political voices on the left were denouncing imperialism in principle, there was little ideological anti-colonialism in France. It did not become an article of faith among French Socialists as it did in the British Labour Party. There was, though, a widespread recognition that the fiction of assimilation could not be sustained. The new approach (towards which French policy makers had in fact been edging even before the war) was that of *association*. This, as the name implies, lay a little closer to the more distanced British approach to colonial rule. Rather than being absorbed into a uniform 'Frenchness', the peoples of the colonies would enter into a kind of bilateral relationship with the colonial power. This, with its symbiotic distribution of benefits, was in fact close to the model Frederick Lugard had described in the 1920s. The main point of departure from the thinking of *The Dual Mandate*, however, lay in France's unbreakable devotion to centralization. There would be few effective attempts at indirect rule in the French colonies. Even within the association arrangements, Paris would control colonial government.

If *association* was designed to save French colonialism after the philosophical dead-end of *assimilation*, it signally failed. Expelled from south-east Asia in the mid-1950s, then almost immediately locked in the long and vicious colonial war in Algeria, France made little effort to hold on to its sub-Saharan colonies. Almost all of French West and Equatorial Africa became independent in the early 1960s. The integrationist mindset had its after-echoes, however. Just as Britain's approach to colonialism was later reflected in the idea of a multicultural

Almost all of French West and Equatorial Africa became independent in the early 1960s.

Commonwealth, France's post-colonial relationships have been shaped by the philosophical foundations of its centralizing, monocultural imperial project.

Portugal: 'one state, single and indivisible'

Further along the philosophical scale towards the extreme of colonial integrationism lay Portugal. Portugal's twentieth-century colonialism has been the source of much curiosity, even bewilderment, to outsiders. Here was a country whose own social and economic indicators in the 1960s and early 1970s placed it on the borderlines of Third World status. Yet, long after the developed, industrialized countries of Western Europe had divested themselves of their colonies, Portugal clung on to huge expanses of Africa. It did so by its fingernails, fighting guerrilla wars with nationalist movements in all three of its major African colonies – Angola, Mozambique and Guinea-Bissau. In Portugal's own official estimation even in the last days of its empire, however, its policies were both rational and principled. The Portuguese presence throughout the world, according to the authoritarian regime that ruled the country until the revolution of 1974, was part of a sacred national 'vocation' (*vocação nacional*). From the 1930s to the 1970s the governments of António de Oliveira Salazar and his successor Marcello Caetano saw metropolitan Portugal and its *ultramar* (literally 'overseas') as a seamless garment woven from the threads of language, culture and history.

One piece of official iconography encapsulates this idea. Throughout the Salazar years every school classroom in Portugal and Portuguese Africa had the same map pinned to its wall. It showed metropolitan Portugal welded to Angola, Mozambique and Guinea-Bissau in Africa, and East Timor and Goa in Asia. This was superimposed over a map of Europe, dwarfing the rest of the continent. The caption was *Portugal não é um País Pequeno* – 'Portugal is not a Small Country'. The nation therefore was not in reality a poor, underdeveloped fragment clinging to the periphery of Europe. It was not destined by geography and history to lie in the perpetual shadow of Spain, its equally underdeveloped but much larger neighbour. On the contrary, 'Portugal' was a vast, varied and rich slice of the planet. There was an obvious psychological similarity here between Portuguese and the French colonial motivations. But while France gloried in its imperial status in reaction to specific humiliations of European politics and war, Portugal's imperial neediness was less focused on events. It was continuous and deeply rooted in a centuries-old culture.

Ironically, Portugal found itself as a major twentieth-century colonial actor almost by accident. While Britain, France and Germany engaged with the 'new imperialism' of the late nineteenth century because of their economic and industrial power, Portugal's involvement was in many ways defensive and opportunistic. Ports and harbours on the coasts of Africa had serviced traffic to Portugal's First (Asian) and Second (Brazilian) Empires since the end of the fifteenth century. But although long-established, Portugal's presence in Africa was tenuous in the mid-nineteenth century. Some plantation agriculture and much slave-trading had taken Portuguese settlers and adventurers inland at times, but there was little consistent colonization or effective occupation. Now the sudden scramble for African territory by its northern European neighbours brought both a threat and an opportunity for Portugal. The threat was of displacement by richer and better-resourced European rivals. But the scramble also held out the opportunity for Portugal to attach itself to the larger movement by asserting its prior 'ownership' of African lands and effectively establishing a Third Empire. In the event, the threat failed to materialize and the opportunity was exploited. This was made possible by the fact that Portugal's continued presence in Africa was useful to the manoeuvrings of the other powers involved in the scramble. In this way Portugal rejoined the ranks of imperialist powers and throughout most of the twentieth century Africa dominated Portuguese politics, diplomacy and public imagination to a degree unimaginable in the larger imperialist countries.

Salazar's *Estado Novo* (authoritarian Portugal's supposed 'New State') drew national self-esteem from the possession of large tropical colonies. The colonial empire provided a distraction from the larger Portuguese reality of economic underdevelopment and cultural stagnation that had long prevented the country from making any impact on the European mainstream. Philosophical rationalization was found in the construction of a 'pluricontinentalist' mythology. This underpinned an extreme integrationist view of empire which defined Portuguese colonialism by denying its existence. There were really no colonies, just 'one state, single and indivisible' (*um estado, uno e indivisível*). The guru of this so-called 'luso-tropicalism' was Gilberto Freyre who, significantly perhaps, was not himself Portuguese but Brazilian. Freyre wrote of the quality of the Portuguese language itself as a catalyst and adhesive of a unique '*pax lusitania*'. His best-known work, *O Mundo que os Português Criou* (*The World that the Portuguese Created*), published in 1940, was quickly adopted by the Salazar regime as a semi-official statement of Portugal's national ideology.

After the Second World War, as Britain began to contemplate withdrawal from its colonies and France – for a time at least – fought against the tide to avoid doing so, Africa continued to provide a key part of Portugal's self-identity. Emerging from wartime neutrality and tainted by its association with European fascism, the comfort of empire was more necessary than ever. At the same time, however, colonialism was under increasing international threat. The new United Nations was unwilling to leave Portugal to pursue its own mythical destiny and rejected Lisbon's refusal to accept the basic principle of colonial self-determination. In response, Salazar adjusted the national constitution to identify the colonies formally as 'overseas provinces' (*províncias ultramarinas*). This gave a spurious legal rationalization to the pluricontinental myth. 'Independence' for Angola or Mozambique would, in this constitutional formulation, be as meaningless as 'independence' for Oporto or the Algarve. All were integral parts of the nation. The move failed utterly to convince anyone outside Portugal, but within the country itself integrationism remained a credible and popular policy. There were, after all, about three-quarters of a million white settlers in Angola and Mozambique for whom the idea of forming part of an extended nation was far preferable to any thought of African independence.

Inevitably, reality impinged. In April 1974, after thirteen years of colonial war in Africa, the Portuguese military itself moved against the regime. Little more than a year later the 500-year-old Portuguese empire had disappeared. It did so amidst some odd ironies. It is possible that a sort of 'Portuguese Africa' might have survived longer if Lisbon had not insisted on applying its ultra-integrationist philosophy to its logical conclusion. The most intense war took place in Guinea-Bissau, which was not a colony of settlement and, being economically unproductive, could hardly be described as a colony of exploitation either. An accommodation with the nationalists there might just have eased the situation in the large and important colonies of settlement Angola and Mozambique. But the regime insisted on fighting to retain Guinea at whatever cost. It was, after all, part of the indivisible whole. This proved to be a principle too far for the beleaguered Portuguese army, which called time on the entire colonial project.

Intriguingly, that same army, radicalized during the process of the revolution in 1974 and 1975, had its own vision of a post-colonial pluricontinental Portugal. In this, the metropolis would lie at the centre of a new community of radical socialist states tied together by their common luso-tropical heritage. Integration still, but cast in the setting of revolutionary solidarity rather than European imperialism. It was a quixotic dream. The reality was that, once divested of its empire, newly democratic Portugal could join the European mainstream, exclusion from which had driven it to its peculiar vision of empire in the first place. For their part, the new 'Afro-Marxist' states created in the wake of Portugal's departure held on to the language but quickly and systematically rooted out every other remnant of the luso-tropical myth.

The differing doctrines that guided the colonialisms of Britain, France and Portugal have left their traces in contemporary attitudes and relationships. It is not just language that tells a visitor whether they are in Angola, Senegal or Kenya; Singapore, Laos or East Timor. To live and work in Mozambique in the late 1970s after independence was to survive a nightmare of bureaucracy which made Alice's journey through the looking glass seem effortless and logical. But this was not principally the effect, as often claimed, of the sudden imposition of Soviet-style communism. On the contrary, it was a result of the persistence of the old centralizing

> *To live and work in Mozambique in the late 1970s after independence was to survive a nightmare of bureaucracy which made Alice's journey through the looking glass seem effortless and logical.*

mindset of the Portuguese colonial state, now without even the limited efficiency of the Portuguese state itself. Similarly, the politics and governance of, say, Benin and Ghana differ radically not by accident, but as a result of ideas, attitudes and systems put in place long before even the independence of these countries.

Recommended reading

The philosophical bases of British colonialism are dealt with by David Armitage in *The Ideological Origins of the British Empire* (Cambridge: Cambridge University Press, 2000). Frederick Lugard's own account of British indirect rule in West Africa is set out in his famous *The Dual Mandate in British Tropical Africa* (London: Blackwood, 1922). His life and times are presented in rather hagiographical detail by his biographer Dame Margery Perham. Volume I of her huge work covers *The Years of Adventure, 1858–1898* while volume II deals with *The Years of Authority, 1898–1945* (London: Collins, 1956 and 1960). The second volume is the more important in respect of Lugard's approach to colonial administration.

The different approaches to the advocacy and presentation of the colonial project in Britain and France are compared by Thomas G. August in *The Selling of the Empire: British and French Imperial Propaganda, 1890–1940* (Westport, CT: Greenwood Press, 1985).

A recent book by Raymond F. Betts deals specifically with the two successive French doctrines of colonial rule: *Assimilation and Association in French Colonial Theory* (Lincoln, NE: University of Nebraska Press, 2006). Frantz Fanon's two classic studies of French colonialism from the 'receiving end' have rarely been out of print, even in translation. They are: *Black Skin, White Masks* (London: Pluto, 1986) and *The Wretched of the Earth* (London: Penguin, 2001).

Little has been written in English (or translated into it) on Portugal's colonial philosophies. *Portuguese Africa: A Handbook* (London: Pall Mall, 1969), edited by David M. Abshire and Michael A. Samuels, was published just as the endgame of Portugal's colonialism was getting under way and provides several insights into Portuguese thinking. So, too, from a distinctly unsympathetic perspective, does Basil Davidson's chapter, 'Portuguese-Speaking Africa', in volume VIII of *The Cambridge History of Africa (From c. 1940 to c. 1975)* (Cambridge: Cambridge University Press, 1984).

CHAPTER 5

Colonialism after the Second World War: the cold war and the United Nations

THE SECOND WORLD WAR, like the First, had a profound effect on Europe's colonial empires. Post-1918 conditions changed the position of colonialism in the international relations of the time. The world shaped by the 1939–45 conflict was one in which the basic idea of colonialism rapidly lost international credibility. A number of political, social and economic forces quickly eroded the bases on which colonial relationships had been founded. These were the 'push' and 'pull' factors that determined the arrival of decolonization and propelled formal European political power from the global South.

This did not take place within a straightforward sequence of events, however. The different European imperialist countries had markedly different relationships with their respective territories in the final stage of the colonial period. These differences were shaped largely by the contrasting colonialist philosophies held by the various imperial powers. The same imperial state might relate in contrasting ways to different colonies within its own empire. France's traumatic final years in Algeria contrasted with the relative ease of decolonization in French West Africa. Britain found it much easier to slip away from Ghana than it did from Rhodesia. But within a decade of the end of the Second World War the writing on the wall for colonialism was clear. Within the second decade the process of decolonization was at its peak. Within three decades it was all but finished.

If the war itself helped to fashion the coffin of European colonialism, post-war conditions provided the setting for a rapid burial. The cold war, which set in almost immediately peace had been declared in 1945, accelerated the retreat from empire. Global bipolarity and the battle of ideas that supposedly underlay it saw the 'new' west – the United States – at odds with the 'old' west – the European colonial powers. The Americans pressed their weaker, more dependent European allies to free the alliance of the political vulnerability that their continuing colonial policies created.

The cold war, which set in almost immediately peace had been declared in 1945, accelerated the retreat from empire.

The world organizations of the post-1945 period, which became arenas for many cold war battles, also had a major role in speeding the end of empire. Just as the League of Nations had mediated a new international morality after the First World War, now the United Nations became the moral voice of a yet newer world order after the Second. The League mandate system was a radical departure from a past in which colonies were simple commodities that changed hands between losers and winners after wars. The UN took the process a critical stage further. Now, self-determination was to be seen as a near destination rather than a long-term aspiration.

The United Nations also provided a welcoming embrace when the former colonies reached that destination. Rather than being cast adrift in a predatory international system after the departure of their colonial masters, the new states found space in the UN General Assembly for the development of what amounted to a diplomatic self-help association. The UN and the early experience of international cooperation it gave to the new post-colonial states provided a firm launch pad for a range of Third World organizations which in the 1960s and 1970s would further speed the end of the imperial age. More concretely, in its first decades the UN's military peacekeeping capacity was devoted mainly to crises with their roots in European colonialism, from the Middle East and South Asia to Central Africa.

The 'push' from the colonies and the 'pull' back to Europe

What were the principal forces pushing the European colonialists from their possessions after 1945? How did the war alter the balance of the relationship between colonizer and colonized? The Second World War, much more than the First, was a conflict of ideas. National self-determination became part of the rhetoric of the First World War only late in the day. And when it came it was carefully restricted to the European parts of the defeated empires rather than their distant colonial possessions which remained under European control, albeit as League mandates.

In contrast, the war of 1939–45 was a truly global struggle at the end of which the principles of democracy and independence could not be geographically limited. In both wars, colonial conscripts had been pushed into the front line in defence of 'freedom'. In 1945, however, they were quicker to make the obvious connection between this freedom and the colonial domination to which their imperial masters expected them quietly to return. Nationalism had been growing throughout the European colonial empires in the interwar years and it was encouraged by the new morality embodied in the League of Nations. After 1945 this increasing political confidence in the colonies had been hardened by participation in the global struggle for democracy. As a result, the European powers were now under pressure to, putting it bluntly, put their ideological money where their wartime rhetoric had been.

There was another dimension to the pressure for fundamental change in the colonies. The allies had not won the war with ease. The political and military weakness of the colonial empires had been exposed. The myth of imperial vulnerability was no longer sustainable. France, Belgium and the Netherlands were themselves defeated and occupied, in a form of imperialism by Nazi Germany. Britain, although not subjected to this ultimate humiliation, had been tested to the limit and some fundamental weaknesses had been revealed. In French Africa and in France's Arab mandates the Nazi puppet Vichy regime and Free French forces tussled with each other for control. In the Congo, colonial authority was dramatically weakened during Belgium's wartime occupation by Germany. The nascent colonial nationalist movements would obviously draw lessons from this faltering of imperial power.

The pomp of European imperial authority was most thoroughly destroyed in Asia. Japanese forces had swept through the Asia-Pacific region pushing aside the supposed might of the colonial powers. Britain was unceremoniously ejected from Malaya, Burma and Hong Kong. India, the jewel in the imperial crown, came under threat. The vast archipelago of the Dutch East Indies was occupied with ease by the Japanese, as was French Indo-China. The European colonial masters fled or were interned by the Japanese in the most humiliating circumstances. The re-occupation of these territories when it came was as a result not of resurgent European power but through the defeat of Japan by the United States. Anti-colonial nationalism had already been more developed in Asia than in Africa even before the war. In the French territories, existing nationalist movements had shifted their hostility to the new Japanese imperialists during the years of occupation. They were hardly going to submit meekly to re-colonization by their European masters, having just helped defeat the Japanese. Both France and Holland were slow to recognize how utterly changed the situation was. They were forced to navigate a steep learning curve at the end of which lay their expulsion from Asia.

The physical vulnerability of the European powers, along with the military and political potential of the nationalist movements, therefore altered fundamentally the rules of colonial engagement. The newly confident nationalists of Asia and Africa were now empowered to construct new futures. It is one of the great paradoxes of colonialism that they did so

> *The newly confident nationalists of Asia and Africa were now empowered to construct new futures.*

using the political forms that the colonizers themselves had brought. Universal franchise, republicanism, territorial state-hood and international sovereignty were essentially western ideas that had travelled to Asia and Africa in the hand baggage of the imperialists themselves. These ideas had now become the nemesis of the colonialism that had introduced them.

Of course, it is impossible to fully separate the dynamics of the colonial push and the metropolitan pull from empire. But this resurgent colonial nationalism was certainly complemented by the domestic conditions Europe had to confront after 1945. The war had exposed not just European weakness in Africa and Asia; it had enfeebled Europe itself. Britain, France, Belgium and Holland emerged from the conflict in a state of near economic collapse. Just as the United States had been the critical factor in the expulsion of Japan from Europe's Asian colonies, American intervention in the form of the Marshall Plan was crucial to Europe's own post-war reconstruction. In this situation Europe's persisting imperial pretensions seemed not just mis-placed but self-destructive. Colonial administration was expensive and the economic returns to metropolitan economies from their formal empires were uncertain at best.

For some in Europe there were lessons in Turkey's renais-sance as a self-contained nation-state with the end of the Ottoman Empire after the First World War. In this view, national efforts ought to be devoted to the absolute priority of recon-struction within Europe's own borders. More commonly, the mood was one of thoughtfulness. Anti-colonialist politics in Europe developed after 1945 in a way unthinkable after 1918. The Labour Party in Britain and socialists in Belgium and the Netherlands (though not to the same extent in France) began to commit themselves to colonial withdrawal. Political ground previously occupied by the Communists and far-left was increasingly taken over by the mainstream parties of the centre-left. The Wilsonian moral imperative of colonial self-determination, never entirely adopted even by liberals in Europe after 1918, now became the standard progressive position.

It was helpful here that liberals and socialists in continental Europe had another political project to occupy them. European integration offered both short-term gains in the form of economic reconstruction, and a longer-term vision of a transformed, conflict-free continent. Colonialism was not merely irrelevant to the new ideal of a united Europe; it was a threat to its realization. Pragmatism and ideology thus came together. The representation of empire as a 'burden' to an enfeebled Europe became entwined with the end of empire as a moral imperative. Although this may not have been the predominant feature of the new pan-European thinking, it did contribute to the emergence of a new political culture across the western part of the continent.

The cold war and the death throes of colonialism: the Suez crisis

The speed and completeness with which the cold war descended on the post-1945 international system took most people by surprise. Ideological tension between the Soviet Union and the western allies was plain even before the end of the Second World War, but few would have predicted the degree to which it would come to dominate the international relations of the second half of the twentieth century. Inevitably, the cold war and its division of the world between the two poles of Washington and Moscow became entangled with the last phase of colonialism.

This entanglement highlighted the internal division within the western alliance itself between 'anti-colonial' America and the residual imperialism of its European allies. For the Americans, European colonialism was a major chink in the west's armour in the global battle for the moral high ground, a tactical gift to the Soviet Union. In the hands of Moscow's propagandists it could be presented as the ultimate hypocrisy behind the west's claims to be the only true champions of democracy and national independence.

The sharpest illustration of this western dilemma came in 1956 with the crisis triggered by Egypt's nationalization of the Suez Canal.

The sharpest illustration of this western dilemma came in 1956 with the crisis triggered by Egypt's nationalization of the Suez Canal. Egypt's charismatic nationalist leader, Gammal Abdel Nasser, had developed a grand plan to build a high dam on the Nile at Aswan. This was designed to produce hydro-electricity in quantities that would revolutionize Egypt's industrial development and social modernization. It was a totemic project of post-imperial development. The Americans, however, had become anxious about Nasser's closeness to the Soviet Union. They therefore sought to nudge Egypt's foreign policy in a more 'acceptable' direction. To this end World Bank financing of the Aswan project was withdrawn. If this was designed to pull Egypt back into line with the west it proved to be a disastrous miscalculation. Nasser was not to be intimidated, and denounced the threat to the Aswan scheme as imperialist bullying. The one piece of international leverage that he could exert was Egypt's power over the Suez Canal. Consequently, Nasser announced its nationalization when support was withdrawn from the Aswan scheme in July 1956.

The canal was originally built by the French engineer Ferdinand de Lesseps and remained the property of an Anglo-French consortium. It had been constructed in the 1860s within a complex but essentially colonial relationship between the two European powers and Egypt. The waterway became indispensable to the colonial outreach of both countries. It linked the Mediterranean directly to the Red Sea, giving access from Europe to the Indian Ocean without the need to circumnavigate the African continent. The canal therefore provided an infinitely faster, safer and more economical route to the Asian colonies. Later, as Europe became increasingly dependent on oil, it provided direct access to the wells of the Persian Gulf. However, for Egyptian nationalists, as long as it remained under foreign control, the canal was a symbol of their country's semi-colonial status. Its nationalization therefore served more than one purpose for Nasser. Income from passage fees would help cover the hole blown in the funding of the Aswan project by America's punitive action. It was also a radical assertion of post-colonial sovereignty.

Gamal Abdel Nasser (1918–1970)

Nasser was born in impoverished circumstances in Alexandria, though his formative years involved frequent moves around Egypt because of his father's employment as a minor government official. From an early age he was active in protests against the

British presence in Egypt and its influence over its government. After leaving school he entered military college, graduating as a junior officer at a critical point in the development of Egyptian nationalism. In 1952 he was part of a group of nationalist army officers who overthrew the corrupt, pro-British monarchy. Two years later, after considerable intrigue and manoeuvring, Nasser emerged from the military collective as the clear national leader. He came to international prominence in 1956 when his nationalization of the Suez Canal led to an Anglo-French invasion and war with Israel. The Suez affair confirmed Nasser at the head of the larger pan-Arab movement. In pursuit of the dream of Arab unification he negotiated the creation of the United Arab Republic (UAR) in 1958. This joined Egypt with Syria in what was supposed to be the first stage in the grand scheme for a single Arab state. Syria's withdrawal from the arrangement in 1961 did nothing to lessen Nasser's standing in the region. Beyond the Middle East he was a key architect of the global non-aligned movement. In 1967 he launched the attack on Israel that triggered the so-called Six Day War. Despite a humiliating defeat in this conflict, he stayed in power until his death in 1970. His reputation in the Middle East remained high for many years after this, though it has been somewhat overshadowed by the more recent rise of Islamism as the main expression of radicalism in the region.

It was not the United States that reacted most violently to the nationalization but Britain and France. Between them the British Conservative prime minister, Anthony Eden, and his French Socialist counterpart, Guy Mollet, concocted a plan with Israel to justify an invasion of Egypt and force the return of the canal to their control. Israel was invited to attack Egypt on the pretext of responding to cross-border guerrilla raids, which it did at the end of October 1956. An Anglo-French force then intervened to 'stabilize' the situation following Egypt's (wholly predictable) refusal to withdraw from the canal zone.

It was an imperial reflex on a grand scale and an unmitigated disaster for the conspirators. The United States had been kept in the dark about Anglo-French intentions and President Dwight D. Eisenhower and his Secretary of State John Foster Dulles, normally an implacable 'cold warrior', were furious. More important than the *lèse majesté* of the Europeans' failure to consult with Washington was the damage done by the adventure to the west's cold war diplomacy. In particular, it had distracted international attention from the Soviet Union's brutal suppression of an uprising in Hungary (one of Moscow's own 'colonies' acquired in the aftermath of the Second World War). More generally, the Americans were keenly aware of the damage post-imperial rampages like the Suez invasion would do to the west's credibility in a world that was becoming ever more anti-colonial in its assumptions and expectations.

American pressure on Britain (including a threat to undermine sterling on the money markets) brought the Eden government to heel. Frantic behind-the-scenes activity in the United Nations by its Swedish secretary-general Dag Hammarskjöld and the Canadian foreign minister Lester Pearson, encouraged by the United States, led to a settlement built round the intervention of a UN peacekeeping force and a simultaneous Anglo-French withdrawal. Putting as brave a face on these developments as

The view throughout the world was quite clear: the old colonial dinosaurs had thrashed their tails and had only speeded their extinction as a result.

possible, the British and French suggested that their intervention had been designed merely to hold the ring pending just such multilateral action. This convinced nobody. The view throughout the world was quite clear: the old colonial dinosaurs had thrashed their tails and had only speeded their extinction as a result. In the future, British prime ministers might still invade Arab countries, but only in coalition with the United States, not in conflict with its interests.

The Suez affair provided a weathervane of changing political and public opinion in Europe itself. In Britain (though less so in France which was still largely united behind its imperial role) the crisis polarized opinion. The cleavage was not simply one between the Conservative government and the Labour opposition. Many forward-looking Conservatives were shocked at the imperial insouciance of their prime minister's behaviour as well, and despaired of the consequences for Britain's place in the post-1945 international system. Within months Eden had resigned, irreparably damaged by the affair. His supporters insisted that the historical back-story to his action was the rise of Hitler (Eden had been a vocal anti-appeaser in the 1930s) and not imperial arrogance. This may have had some substance, but it was perception, both in Britain and abroad, that was important. This was one of anachronistic colonial arrogance, utterly unsuited to the new terms on which international relations were to be conducted.

It is wrong to say, as some have, that the Suez affair was a trigger to the collapse of European imperialism. The retreat from empire was determined long before 1956. However, the crisis provided an occasion for reflection by those who continued to think that Europe might still have the capacity to maintain its colonial role. The 'west' was now defined primarily as one pole in a bipolar world; it was no longer a synonym for imperial power. This was brought home repeatedly to the Europeans by the United States over the next decade. The pressures exerted, for example, on Portugal to extricate itself from Africa may not have been as sharp and direct as those applied over Suez, and America's own activities during the cold war in Latin America and south-east Asia might themselves be reasonably described as 'colonialist'. Nevertheless, the drift was clear: European colonialism and the cold war could not be pursued together.

The United Nations and 'trusteeship'

The United Nations intervention in Suez was part of a much broader engagement by the organization with the colonial and new post-colonial world. When the UN supplanted the League in 1945 it was understandable that the new, hopeful, world organization would seek to create as much distance as possible between itself and its discredited predecessor. In reality the UN was a very similar institution to the League, both in form and function. Its basic structure of Security Council, General Assembly and Secretariat was almost identical to that of the League. So was its fundamental purpose: the establishment of a comprehensive system of collective security. But for the UN, much more than for the League, the 'problem' of colonialism was a major obstruction to be negotiated on the road to this goal.

One of the many responsibilities that the UN inherited directly from the League was the mandate system. Nomenclature changed here as elsewhere in the succession process between the two organizations: the Mandates Commission became the

Trusteeship Council. The altered terminology was not perhaps merely cosmetic in this case. The word 'trusteeship' carried a stronger connotation of 'transition', of a process leading to the final conclusion of self-determination and independence. Although this had been implicit in the idea of a 'mandate', now, a crucial quarter of a century later, it was made more explicit. This was clear in Article 73 of the UN Charter (the succeeding document to the League Covenant). This provided a general introduction to the trusteeship system presented in the form of a 'Declaration Regarding Non-Self-Governing Territories'. It signalled a departure from the League's stance on colonialism in a very significant sense by referring to *all* 'territories whose peoples have not yet attained a full measure of self-government'. The UN, therefore, took on itself a responsibility not just for those territories it had inherited as League mandates with some post-Second World War additions. The Declaration claimed a role for the organization in the policies, practices and plans for the colonial empires even of the wartime victors.

This suggested a new limitation on the sovereign rights of imperial powers over their colonies. Those powers were now required to

recognize the principle that the interests of the inhabitants of these territories are paramount, and accept as a sacred trust the obligation to promote to the utmost, within the system of international peace and security established by the present Charter, the well-being of the inhabitants of these territories.

A list of specific undertakings to be accepted by the imperial powers then follows. There was to be 'due respect for the culture of the peoples concerned, their political, economic, social, and educational advancement, their just treatment, and their protection against abuses'. 'Self-government' was to be developed, taking 'due account of the political aspirations of the peoples, and to assist them in the progressive development of their free political institutions, according to the particular circumstances of each territory and its peoples and their varying stages of advancement'. Finally, all imperial powers were to report regularly to the UN secretary-general on the economic, social and educational conditions in each of their colonies.

The Declaration did not have a trouble-free birth. The idea for it began, as much in the Charter did, among American planners. The original intention was to require a concrete commitment from all colonial powers to bring their territories to independence. Winston Churchill, on behalf of Britain, strongly objected to the use of the term 'independence'. So, even more strongly, did France. The principle of *assimilation* might have become discredited as the basis of a distinctly French colonial philosophy by this stage, but its successor, *association*, still did not recognize the desirability, let alone the inevitability, of the end of empire. A transatlantic compromise was therefore reached by which the term 'independence' was replaced by 'self-government' in the Declaration.

Despite this disagreement over terminology (admittedly not a trivial one), the inclusion of the Declaration in the UN Charter marked the acceptance of a new international reality by the imperial powers. Henceforward, colonialism, by whatever state, would not be accepted as a fixed and permanent feature of the international system. Only diehard Portugal, which regarded its colonies as simple extensions – territorial and spiritual – of the motherland, balked at the idea. However, weak and marginalized as it was, the Portuguese regime could do nothing to alter the new trend of thinking.

Fourteen articles of the UN Charter (75 to 88) were devoted to the trusteeship arrangements which replaced the League mandate system. The new scheme increased international authority over the territories for which the UN had special responsibility. The Trust Territories, as the former mandates were now called, were subject to a greater degree of UN oversight than under the League. But in one very significant respect the system fell far short of the original intentions of American President Franklin D. Roosevelt (whose moral vision in the construction of the UN was comparable to that of Woodrow Wilson in the establishment of the League). The Declaration Regarding Non-Self-Governing Territories, though very radical in its way, was in fact something of a compromise covering a retreat from a much grander vision.

Roosevelt had originally proposed that the Trusteeship system should embrace *every* colonial territory. That is to say, there would be no British, French, Portuguese or other 'empires' but instead a series of UN administered trusteeships, secondary responsibility for which might, or might not, reside with their former colonial masters. This was a step too far for those colonial powers that had emerged as victors in the war and were therefore in a position to argue. Churchill in particular was outraged, and denounced the idea 'that the British Empire is to be put into the dock and examined by everyone' (Ruth Russell, *History of the UN Charter* [1958], p. 541). At the same time, Roosevelt came under pressure from his own generals. American military planners wanted to use the ex-Japanese territories in the Pacific, which were about to become American Trusteeships, as strategic outposts. It was not, therefore, in the American interest to spread UN authority too far across the colonial world.

Despite this shortfall in its original ambitions, the United Nations still managed to construct a powerful role for itself in the colonial world. It is right to emphasize, though, that the UN was building here

Despite this shortfall in its original ambitions, the United Nations still managed to construct a powerful role for itself in the colonial world.

on ground first prepared by the League. Like the League in the 1920s, the post-war United Nations both fostered and reflected a new international sensibility towards colonialism. The UN's engagement with the issue came at the point of endgame, however. During the 1960s and 1970s the organization became midwife to what was in essence a new international system.

UN forces, colonialism and the cold war

The Emergency Force, established in 1956 to help deal with the Suez crisis, was the first large-scale UN peacekeeping operation. It was called into being to deal with a conflict with deep colonial roots which also had immediate implications for the conduct of the cold war. Crises of colonialism and of the cold war – frequently intermeshed – provided the *raisons d'être* of peacekeeping until the 1990s.

Suez was not the first occasion on which the UN had used military units in a crisis that had grown from European imperialism. Smaller-scale observer operations had already been put in place in two post-colonial flashpoints in the late 1940s. In 1948 and 1949 military monitoring missions were sent to oversee ceasefires after conflicts that had been sparked by difficult transitions from colonial relationships. The first of these was in

Palestine, where in 1948 Britain withdrew from the League of
Nations mandate it had accepted after the end of the Ottoman
empire. The competing and apparently incompatible demands of
Arab nationalism on one side and Zionist pressure for the creation of a Jewish state on the other simply became too much for
an exhausted post-war Britain to manage. The British withdrawal in May 1948 was immediately followed by the declaration
of the state of Israel, and by the first of the tragic sequence of
Arab–Israeli wars that punctuated the rest of the twentieth
century. The second UN intervention at this time followed a war
between the new states of India and Pakistan over the border
territory of Kashmir (the national and religious origins of which
were described in the last chapter). Self-evidently, from the
vantage point of the twenty-first century, neither of these UN
missions brought a long-term solution. Both conflicts persisted
undiminished in ferocity more than half a century later. But the
UN's objectives at the beginning of the crises were modest.
Judged within these aims the operations made a real contribution to – and set an important precedent for – the management
of tensions emerging from post-colonial adjustments that the
colonial power itself was unable to resolve.

Patrice Lumumba (1925–1961)

Lumumba was born in the Kasai province of the Belgian Congo
and educated in a Protestant mission school. Moving to the
colonial capital Léopoldville, he followed the route of many other
nationalist leaders across the colonial world by finding work in
the colonial administration. In Léopoldville he became a trade
union activist. This brought him into contact with anti-colonial
leaders in other African colonies, and in 1958 he founded the

Congolese Nationalist Movement (MNC) whose policies were shaped by the larger pan-Africanist project. In 1959 the Belgian government suddenly announced that the Congo would become independent the following year. Reluctantly, the Belgians recognized that they would have to negotiate with Lumumba, despite their intense dislike of him and his politics, as the MNC was now a major force in the territory. Lumumba became prime minister of the new Congo republic in June 1960. Chaos quickly overtook the infant state as the lack of preparedness for independence took its toll. Political splits and an army revolt brought a major UN peacekeeping intervention just weeks after independence. Lumumba, with a small and weak ethnic base, fell victim to tribal politics and was ousted from office. His radical leftist rhetoric had made him few friends in western governments and he now found himself isolated and vulnerable. In January 1961 he was captured by his political enemies, transferred to the breakaway province of Katanga and brutally murdered. His death (in which western governments were accused of complicity) created a major cold war crisis in the UN. It also provided a martyr for the radical pan-African cause. This status has endured, despite Lumumba's limited achievements in power.

Palestine and Kashmir marked the beginning of the long narrative of United Nations military intervention in post-colonial conflicts. In 1960 the focus shifted to sub-Saharan Africa when the UN became involved in a huge and complex operation in the former Belgian Congo. Belgium had withdrawn from its vast central African territory in July of that year, having done virtually nothing to prepare it as a viable independent state. Chaos and disintegration followed almost immediately. Belgium, the object of extreme suspicion among the Congolese nationalists who had taken power after independence, intervened to protect European interests. But it had no moral authority to resolve the crisis –

and insufficient capacity to do so in any case. The issue was therefore laid at the door of the United Nations by the Congo's radical young Prime Minister, Patrice Lumumba. Like the Suez force, the Congo operation was very much secretary-general Dag Hammarskjöld's project (it was a commitment that would lead to his death in a plane crash during crisis talks in 1961). Quicker than most to grasp the implications of the end of the European empires for international peace and security, Hammarskjöld realized that, if the Middle East and Asia were the preoccupations of the late 1940s and 1950s, Africa would be the concern of the 1960s. The UN in his view should take a lead role in managing its transition. The peacekeeping operation in the Congo lasted four years and had a high human and material cost. It was not a resounding success. On the international plane, instead of sealing the crisis off from broader rivalries, UN involvement itself became a major source of conflict between the cold war blocs. The Congo's own deep problems, just like those of Palestine and Kashmir, remained unresolved many decades later. It is probable, though, that without the UN presence the crisis of Congo's emergence from colonialism might have consumed many more lives than it did.

Dag Hammarskjöld (1905–1961)

The son of a Swedish prime minister, Hammarskjöld came from the upper echelons of his country's political elite. Having risen quickly through the ranks of the public service he found himself in 1953 as Swedish representative at the United Nations. Following the resignation in that year of the organization's first secretary-general (Norway's Trygve Lie), Hammarskjöld was seen by both eastern and western blocs as the neutral, safe pair of hands necessary to fill the post in the troubled aftermath of the Korean War. He soon proved himself much more of an activist secretary-general than had been anticipated. He was sharply aware of the new tensions that the end of empire was imposing on the international system. He sought to address these through the development of peacekeeping as a means of preventing post-colonial crises from slipping into the dangerous currents of the cold war. He was instrumental in the deployment of peacekeepers during the Suez crisis of 1956, on a smaller scale in Lebanon in 1958 and, most ambitiously, in the chaos following Belgium's hurried exit from the Congo in 1960. It was here in central Africa that he met his death in a plane crash while trying to resolve one of the sequence of crises that drove the Congo conflict. Hammarskjöld is universally regarded as one of the most important figures in the history of the United Nations.

More positively, in the dying days of the cold war Africa saw one of the UN's most successful peacekeeping ventures which brought Namibia to independence in 1990. The United Nations had a particular responsibility here. Namibia's problems went directly back to the early days of the League when, as the former German South West Africa, the territory was mandated to South Africa. Little had been done during the course of the mandate – and later the trusteeship – to confront South Africa's determin-ation to annex Namibia or to force compliance with the rules of the system, and by the 1960s a nationalist guerrilla war had begun in the territory. After years of obstruction and delay by South Africa, a deal was finally constructed by which it would accept Namibian independence with the quid pro quo of the withdrawal of Cuban troops from its northern neighbour Angola. The relatively small UN force sent to implement the process was responsible for organizing, administering and monitoring an election for the new post-independence government and for internal and external security. It was a complex and dangerous task, but it was achieved, and became one of the few clear successes for UN peacekeeping in Africa in the twentieth century.

Peacekeeping in the colonial aftermath during the cold war was not restricted to the familiar imperial landscape of Africa and Asia. It had its application in Europe as well.

Peacekeeping in the colonial aftermath during the cold war was not restricted to the familiar imperial landscape of Africa and Asia. It had its application in Europe as well. The island of Cyprus became independent of Britain in 1960, but by 1964 the elaborate constitution put in place to safeguard the rights of the Turkish minority in a Greek-dominated state had begun to unravel. Inter-communal violence followed and, once again, the former colonial power was not best placed to manage the situation. Four decades later UN soldiers were still deployed between the communities in Cyprus and there was little sign that they would be leaving in the foreseeable future. The problem in Cyprus was not that the peacekeepers failed to resolve the basic conflict. That is not the function of peacekeeping. But the peacemaking process there never made any significant progress. In part, this was because it was a post-colonial problem with no real cold war implications; both Greece and Turkey were part of the western alliance. However, here, as in the other conflicts of decolonization and post-colonial adjustment in which the UN became involved, the judgement should not be based on what the UN may have failed to achieve, but what would have happened if there had been no UN presence at all.

Yet, it would be wrong to ignore a darker side of the UN's involvement with the end of empire. At times the anti-colonial imperative was allowed to distort judgements about natural justice. The performance of the UN in the conflict between Indonesia and the Netherlands over Dutch New Guinea in the early 1960s throws a revealing light on both the extent of the anti-colonial climate of the time and its capacity to produce morally dubious outcomes. In 1962 and 1963, while international attention was focused on its efforts in the Congo, the UN became involved in a unique undertaking which has perhaps had less attention from historians than it deserves. In the late 1940s the Netherlands very reluctantly accepted the impossibility of re-establishing its empire in Asia. The new state of Indonesia, declared by powerful nationalist forces after the expulsion of the Japanese, was an inescapable fait accompli. But the Dutch remained in control of one part of its old East Indian empire: the western half of the island of New Guinea. The people of Irian Jaya, as it was known, were tribal Melanesians rather than Asian like the rest of the Indonesian population. The case for the continued Dutch administration in New Guinea was that the inhabitants and cultures of Irian Jaya had to be protected and nurtured until such time as a meaningful act of self-determination could take place. The colonial presence, however, provoked nationalist outrage in Indonesia which, carefully cultivated by the Sukarno regime, escalated to Indonesian military incursions. To break the deadlock between the two countries, in 1962 the United Nations created a Temporary Executive Authority for the territory supported by an international Security Force. In effect, the organization provided a transitional state which removed Irian Jaya from Dutch control before passing it on to Indonesia the following year.

Sukarno (1901–1970)

Sukarno (universally referred to by that single name) was born in Java, the principal island of the Dutch East Indies archipelago. The son of a village school teacher, he immersed himself in Javanese music and literature as a child. It was a short step from this cultural nationalism to anti-colonial activity. In his twenties he was already regarded by the Dutch authorities as a hardened agitator and suffered imprisonment and internal exile as a result. After the Japanese take-over of the Dutch East Indies in 1942, Sukarno chose to regard the invaders as fellow anti-colonialists rather than imperialists in their own right, and collaborated with the occupation forces. With the defeat of Japan in 1945 he declared the independence of Indonesia and organized resistance to attempts by an enfeebled Holland to re-impose colonial rule. The Netherlands grudgingly recognized the new republic in 1949 with Sukarno as its president. Sukarno had a mercurial and unpredictable temperament, and his control over Indonesia was exercised mainly by the projection of his charismatic personality (despite his grandiose claims to be following a distinctive nationalist ideology). He was a voluble advocate of non-alignment in the new post-colonial world, and the high international profile that this bestowed on him distracted foreign attention from the growing unpopularity of his ineffective, capricious and corrupt rule at home. Having incurred the hostility of the west through his diplomatic flirtation with the communist bloc, and that of his neighbours through his aggressive regional foreign policy, he had few friends when the army moved against him in 1966. In the ensuing bloodletting hundreds of thousands of Indonesian communists who had been associated with his regime were slaughtered. Sukarno himself, now a spent force, was left to live out his remaining years largely ignored by the new military regime.

The venture was operationally successful but morally dubious, to say the least. It revealed the sometimes insufficiently questioning anti-colonialism in the UN at the time. Dutch concerns about the fate of the Irian Jayan people if they were to be handed over to Indonesia were justified. In the following decades their lands and resources were expropriated and exploited by Indonesian migrants and companies, and all protests brutally suppressed. But the notion that an imperial power might have a compelling ethical case for retaining its colonies was anathema in the UN General Assembly in the early 1960s. The best that can be said perhaps is that if Indonesia was to take Irian Jaya – and it was inevitable that it would – it was probably better done through an orderly process put in place by the UN rather than through a campaign of violence.

The end of empire, the cold war and the 'Afro-Asian bloc' in the UN

Beyond the role of UN military forces on the ground in easing the transition from colonialism, the organization also provided an immensely important focal point for the new states that emerged as the empires were dissolved. The changing pattern of membership of the United Nations in its first decades indicates a tectonic shift in geographical representation. In 1945 there were just three African states in the UN and eleven from the Middle East and Asia. About 750 million

The changing pattern of membership of the United Nations in its first decades indicates a tectonic shift in geographical representation.

people (a third of the world's population at that time) remained colonial subjects. Fifteen years later in 1960 the UN had doubled in size and Afro-Asian states now accounted for more than half the total membership. By 1980, which roughly marked the end of the European colonial era, the organization had 150 members. Almost two-thirds of them were from Africa or the Asia-Pacific region.

As each successive post-colonial state joined the UN, it found itself in an ever larger community of shared interests. The General Assembly, which was the main forum for these new members, was a much more influential and significant force in world politics in the 1960s and 1970s than later when it became eclipsed by the big power-dominated Security Council. In these earlier years the General Assembly was the platform for a regiment of charismatic post-colonial leaders. The political and rhetorical skills of Nehru of India, Nasser of Egypt, Sukarno of Indonesia and Nkrumah of Ghana helped build a powerful Afro-Asian bloc in the organization and world politics more generally. They would eventually establish their own Non-Aligned Movement beyond the UN whose mission was to create a third force in the cold war between the poles of east and west.

Within the UN perhaps the most important responsibility of this bloc was the acceleration of the process of imperial dissolution from which they themselves had emerged. One of their major achievements in this was the 'Declaration on the Granting of Independence to Colonial Countries and Peoples' which was adopted as a resolution of the General Assembly in December 1960. Debated against the background of the deepening crisis in the Congo, the Declaration took as its starting point 'that the process of liberation is irresistible and irreversible and that, in

order to avoid serious crises, an end must be put to colonialism
...' It was in essence a revision of the original 'Declaration
Regarding Non-Self-Governing Territories' in the UN Charter.
But while the radicalism of the 1945 Declaration lay in its asser-
tion of international oversight of colonial policies, the 1960
resolution simply demanded the end of colonialism:

*The subjection of peoples to alien subjugation, domination and exploit-
ation constitutes a denial of fundamental human rights, is contrary to
the Charter of the United Nations and is an impediment to the promotion of world peace and co-operation.*

*All peoples have the right to self-determination; by virtue of that
right they freely determine their political status and freely pursue their
economic, social and cultural development.*

The increasingly familiar *apologia* for colonialism in the post-war
years, that the subject peoples were simply not 'ready' for independence, was given short shrift: '(i)nadequacy of political,
economic, social or educational preparedness should never serve
as a pretext for delaying independence'. Instead,

*immediate steps shall be taken in ... territories which have not yet
attained independence, to transfer all powers to the peoples of those territories, without any conditions or reservations, in accordance with their freely
expressed will and desire, without any distinction as to race, creed or
colour, in order to enable them to enjoy complete independence and freedom.*

It was a remarkable document in many respects, and the
terms of its adoption said much about the emerging anti-colonialist zeitgeist of the time. Eighty-nine votes were cast in
favour and none against. There were only nine abstentions,
mainly the 'usual suspects' of the dwindling colonial camp:

Belgium, Britain, France, Portugal and Spain along with South Africa. The United States abstained rather than, as had been expected, voting with the majority (reportedly its abstention followed a behind-the-scenes appeal from Britain). The fact that this American abstention took the UN by surprise, however, illustrated a truth about contemporary international politics. As the numbers of independent Afro-Asian states in the world grew with each act of decolonization, so did the urgency with which the two cold war poles courted them. On this occasion the division on the western side (already displayed during the Suez crisis) between the image-conscious United States and the instinctive imperialism of the Europeans ended in a no-score draw. However, this was an exception to the trend of western policy. More usually, the default position was the anti-colonialist one (even when, in the case of Irian Jaya for example, it was not necessarily the morally right one).

Whether or not the emergence of new states from the *political* debris of the European empires was creating a new set of independent *economic* entities was another question, however. It was one that would be posed more urgently as the 1960s gave way to the 1970s.

Recommended reading

Evan Luard's two-volume *History of the United Nations* (London: Macmillan, 1982 and 1989) remains the most comprehensive account of the organization's first two decades. Volume I, *The Years of Western Domination 1945–1955*, provides a thorough exploration of the foundation of the UN and the first assertions of the Afro-Asian presence. The relevance of volume 2 to the last phase of colonialism is evident in its subtitle: *The Age of Decolonization, 1955–65*. The contribution of secretary-general Dag Hammarskjöld in easing huge adjustments to the international system brought about by the end of colonialism is well covered in the detailed though rather uncritical study, *Hammarskjöld* (London: Bodley Head, 1973), written by Brian Urquhart, a senior member of his secretariat. The role of UN peacekeeping in this process is covered by Norrie MacQueen in *United Nations Peacekeeping in Africa since 1960* (London: Longman, 2002) and *Peacekeeping and the International System* (London: Routledge, 2006).

Two books, Richard Crockatt's *The Fifty Years War: The United States and the Soviet Union in World Politics 1941–1991* (London: Routledge, 1994) and Peter Calvocoressi's *World Politics 1945–2000* (London: Longman, 2000) explore the impact of the cold war on the post-colonial world. Keith Kyle's book, *Suez* (London: Weidenfeld & Nicolson, 1991), provides a vivid account of a key event of that period.

CHAPTER 6

Decolonization and neocolonialism

WHEN HISTORIANS IN THE FUTURE come to consider the shaping forces of world politics in the second half of the twentieth century, it is a reasonable bet that decolonization will have a much more prominent place than the cold war. Already in the first decade of the twenty-first century this is probably a less controversial prediction than it would have been even a few years ago. Yet, for half a century after 1945 the strategic and ideological competition between east and west was deemed to be the phenomenon that shaped the age. This was understandable when the nuclear wherewithal behind the confrontation between east and west could destroy the planet several times over. A miscalculation in the superpower relationship could indeed be the end of the world. But later a different perspective began to form. Nuclear armageddon had not happened, and the easing of the threat to human existence allowed cooler judgements to be made. Moreover, the fixation on the cold war had obviously been strongest at the centre of the east–west relationship but the intellectual balance of power in the world began to shift as the twentieth century drew to a close. The historical concerns of those parts of the world for which the cold war was happening 'elsewhere' were gradually given more attention. These concerns were less with the distant prospect of nuclear annihilation than with the immediate realities of under-development.

Although cold war bipolarity profoundly affected the shape of the international system at a particular time, it did not have anything like the impact of decolonization on its basic fabric. During the three decades after 1945 the tally of independent states in the world grew by a factor of

> *During the three decades after 1945 the tally of independent states in the world grew by a factor of three.*

three. As a result, the nature and conduct of international relations changed more in a few years than it had in centuries. The mind-maps of the peoples of both the ex-colonial powers and the former subject territories were fundamentally re-drawn. Quite simply, decolonization created a wholly new conception of the political world and everyone's place within it. How far beyond the political – into areas of economic relations and cultural identities – this new conception extended is a question that takes us into more contested areas of debate.

The geography of decolonization

There was a rough pattern to the progress of decolonization across the global South. In the most general terms, it began in the Middle East and then moved eastwards to south Asia and then to south-east Asia. North Africa came next, then sub-

Saharan Africa. Here, the decolonization of West Africa came first, before the process moved on to the east, the centre and the south.

This sequence was determined by a number of factors, one of the most significant of which was the extent and sophistication of the nationalist challenge in different parts of the colonial world. But there were other influences at play. Pressure from European settlers for continued colonial control was a powerful brake on the pace of decolonization in colonies of settlement, for example. Settler interests in southern Africa proved a major obstacle to Britain's smooth withdrawal, with outright white rebellion in Southern Rhodesia just the most dramatic of a series of complications in the region. The strategic importance of some colonies to the security interests of the imperial power could also delay or complicate decolonization. Part at least of Britain's willingness to outstay its welcome in Cyprus lay in the importance of the island's position in the eastern Mediterranean (the independence settlement finally reached permitted the maintenance of British sovereign base areas). Similar considerations applied to both British and French colonies around the Persian Gulf and Indian Ocean. The questionable viability of some territories as independent entities was also a factor. The colonial powers, often with the best of intentions, sought to avoid the creation of microstates which would struggle to survive alone in the international system. Independence therefore came relatively late to much of the Caribbean and South Pacific (in several parts of these regions it has not come at all). Running through all of these factors determining the pace and range of decolonization was, of course, the strength of the basic commitment of the colonial powers to embracing a post-imperial future.

The Middle East and Asia

Almost all of the Middle East that had been subject to League of Nations mandates after the First World War became independent before 1950. This was a mark of the high temperature of Arab nationalism in a region already aggrieved at the withholding of full independence immediately after the defeat of Turkey in 1918. Iraq became a sovereign state in 1932. The French mandates in Lebanon and Syria were disrupted by the Second World War and both countries had achieved a de facto independence before the end of the conflict. At the same time the independent Kingdom of Jordan emerged from a British mandate. Less decorously, the British abandoned the Palestine mandate in 1948. For London the preferred outcome in Palestine would have been an Arab state incorporating a protected Jewish population. As the appalling dimensions of the Nazi Holocaust became clearer in the post-war years, however, international sympathy for surviving European Jewry and the Zionist aspiration for a separate Jewish state in the Middle East grew. Both the United States and the Soviet Union gradually moved behind this 'solution'. No clear international position was ever agreed, however, and Britain moved to free itself from an increasingly thankless and dangerous responsibility. The immediate consequence was the declaration of the state of Israel and the first of an apparently endless sequence of regional wars.

Britain resisted significant nationalist pressure after 1945 in only one part of the Middle East. The port of Aden lies at the bottom of the Arabian peninsula. Located at the point where the Red Sea enters the Indian Ocean, its strategic importance was obvious. This, along with the Marxist (and therefore pro-Soviet) orientation of the main nationalist movement, meant that, uncharacteristically, Britain was ready to fight to retain control in the 1960s. It did so against the prevailing decolonizing tide, and after a short but ugly guerrilla war a settlement was agreed and Aden became the capital of a new independent South Yemen republic in 1967.

Aden – like the somewhat similar case of Cyprus – was significant only because it was untypical. The first real drama of post-war imperial withdrawal, Britain's dismantling of its Indian empire, had happened two decades earlier and had set the tone for the larger process of decolonization. The independence of India and Pakistan in 1947 (along with Ceylon and Burma the following year) was of enormous importance to the future not just of the region but to the course of world politics in the second half of the twentieth century. By the eve of the British withdrawal it was clear that a major gulf separated the nationalist movements in the Hindu and the Muslim parts of the sub-continent. The Congress Party of Mahatma Gandi was poised to take control of the south while the Muslim League led by Mohammed Jinnah dominated the Islamic north. British policy makers calculated that a single post-colonial state would sooner or later descend into sectarian civil war. The obvious means of preventing this was the partition of the sub-continent into two, largely mono-religious independent countries.

The creation of separate sovereignties in India and Pakistan did not prevent horrific levels of social dislocation and violence.

The creation of separate sovereignties in India and Pakistan did not prevent horrific levels of social dislocation and violence. Perhaps as many as fifteen million people became refugees in the territory of the old British Raj, seeking safety across borders with their own religious group. The tragic drama of Indian independence inspired a prolific amount of fiction writing among which Salman Rushdie's allegorical account of the tumult and its longer-term consequences, *Midnight's Children* (1981), is particularly well known. There is no agreed death toll for the communal massacres that accompanied this population exchange, though some calculations have put it as high as a million. Even when relative stability was achieved, the two states entered a relationship of long-term hostility which has marked the regional international relations of south Asia for the past sixty years.

Mohandas (Mahatma) Gandhi (1869–1948)

Gandi was the son of a prosperous Hindu family from Gujrat in northern India where his father was the civic leader of the city of Porbanadar. He studied law at Bombay (Mumbai) and then London University from which he graduated in 1891, later being called to the English bar. After a short period back in India, he practised law in South Africa where he suffered from the crude racism of the place and time. In South Africa Gandhi was already committed to the ideas of civil disobedience and non-violence in pursuit of political objectives. The social and political conditions of South Africa provided abundant opportunity for the exercise of these principles. On his return to India Gandhi became involved in the Indian National Congress, the principal independence movement. Unlike many high-caste members of Congress, Gandhi devoted himself to the struggles of the poorest in Indian society. The title 'Mahatma' ('Great Soul') was given to him by his supporters at this time. Throughout the 1930s he pursued a two-track approach to the independence struggle, campaigning on grassroots issues while engaging in constitutional negotiations with Britain. He was imprisoned during the Second World War because of his Quit India campaign and his supposedly treasonable stance of refusing to support the war. With independence in 1947, Gandhi first resisted and then reluctantly accepted the partition of India (into Hindu India and Muslim Pakistan) as the only way of avoiding cataclysmic inter-communal violence. Gandhi was assassinated in January 1948 by a Hindu extremist enraged by his conciliatory attitude to Pakistan.

The end of Britain's Indian empire had a broader significance for the whole European decolonization process. The perception both in the colonies and at home was that, if Britain, by far the strongest of the European colonial powers after 1945, was prepared to give up India, historically the brightest gem in its imperial crown, then the ground was truly shifting under the colonial world. Events moved quickly in the rest of British Asia. Malaya, the scene of the imperial power's greatest humiliation at Japanese hands during the war, became independent in 1957. Here the process of the transfer of power was delayed by a Communist insurgency which the colonial power was determined to extinguish before departing. There remained only 'special cases'. Britain retained a protectorate over Brunei, an oil-rich fragment of the island of Borneo, until 1984 and in 1999 Hong Kong was returned to China by the terms of the 99-year lease signed in 1898. In neither of these cases had Britain's extended presence been met by any significant nationalist opposition.

Elsewhere in south-east Asia the process was less straightforward. France, deeply reluctant to recognize the inevitable let alone bow to it, remained an intransigent imperialist. The reclamation of the empire was a means by which France tried to salve the injuries to national esteem inflicted by wartime occupation and collaboration. No French government in these years, whether of the left or the right, was willing to go quietly. This imperial self-image proved to be a massively damaging delusion. France's doomed attempt to hold on to Vietnam ended with military rout by the nationalist forces of Ho Chi Minh's Viet Minh movement at Dien Bien Phu in 1954. Henceforward a quasi-colonial role in the south of Vietnam would be assumed by the United States (which would also have catastrophic consequences for both occupier and occupied in the coming years).

Ho Chi Minh (1890–1969)

Although born into rural poverty, Ho's intellectual abilities secured him a secondary education in the Vietnamese city of Hué after which he became a teacher for a short time. Restlessness, however, soon led him to the merchant navy. He travelled around the world for several years and lived for periods in London and Paris. In France he became involved in the left-wing nationalist politics of the Vietnamese community there and in 1920 he joined the French Communist Party. Returning to Asia, Ho formed the Indochinese Communist Party, slipping back into Vietnam in 1930. French repression of anti-colonial activity was draconian, however, and he was soon forced into exile once again, spending several hazardous years in China. The outbreak of the Second World War and Japan's invasion and occupation of Vietnam provided an opportunity for the Vietnamese nationalists. Ho formed the League for the Independence of Vietnam (the Viet Minh), which became a formidable anti-Japanese guerrilla force. With the end of the war, Ho immediately declared the independence of Vietnam. Post-war France, however, sought to reassert its colonial rule and the guerrilla war resumed, ending with the defeat of French forces at Dien Bien Phu in 1954. The division of Vietnam into a communist north led by Ho and a nominally independent but American-controlled south followed. The seeds of the Vietnam war of the 1960s and 1970s were thus sown. The ailing Ho's role in this was carried out largely behind the scenes as he gradually relinquished formal public office. But the continued presence of the revered 'Uncle Ho' was of great importance to communist morale in the struggle. It is possible that his death in 1969 delayed the final resolution of the war. Saigon, the capital of South Vietnam, was renamed Ho Chi Minh City after the communist victory in 1975.

North Africa and the Algerian crisis

French obduracy also set the tone for the troubled decolonization of North Africa. Almost simultaneously with the humiliation of Dien Bien Phu, France faced an uprising in Algeria. The special problems of anti-colonialism in colonies of settlement came into brutally sharp relief here. If India was the jewel of Britain's empire, Algeria had a similar place in French imperial sentiment. British withdrawal, however, was eased by a long history of indirect rule and the absence of any large-scale European settlement. Algeria, in the tradition of French imperial *assimilation*, was tightly integrated with metropolitan France, both administratively and culturally. It was also home to about a million French migrants, the so-called *pieds noirs* (literally 'black feet') who had made the relatively short journey across the Mediterranean over the previous 120 years.

Following the lead set by Algeria in 1954, independence agitation intensified in France's other North African territories, Morocco and Tunisia, which border Algeria to west and east respectively. While this was obviously encouraged by France's evident weakness elsewhere in its empire, the larger North African regional setting was important too. Libya, which lay further along North Africa's Mediterranean seaboard to the east of Tunisia and west of Egypt, had become independent in 1951. It had been taken from Italy during the war and occupied jointly by France and Britain. If France was prepared to preside over the independence of former Italian colonies, nationalist logic ran, it had no grounds to deny statehood to its own colonies in the region. France was wise enough not to become entangled in a colonial war on three fronts, and reached independence agreements with Algeria's neighbours in 1956. But the loss of Algeria simply could not be countenanced in Paris. The Algerian liberation struggle became one of the most vicious conflicts of the post-war decades. A guerrilla war fought in cities, villages and desert was met by the French with systematic repression, extrajudicial killings and the unapologetic use of torture. The Algerian war became a symbol for the world-wide anti-colonial movement of the time, and was the subject of one of the most powerful pieces of political cinema of the past fifty years, Gillo Pontecorvo's *Battle of Algiers* (1966).

Algeria is a marker of the deep impact that the death throes of colonialism could have on politics in Europe. The crisis effectively brought the end of the French Fourth

Algeria is a marker of the deep impact that the death throes of colonialism could have on politics in Europe.

Republic and the return to politics of the wartime Free French leader Charles de Gaulle at the head of the Fifth. By 1958 France had been reduced to a state of extreme political instability by the fallout from the conflict. A military coup was expected daily as the army made clear its frustration with politicians it accused of weakness in the face of the Algerian insurgency. De Gaulle's return to politics, in the role of powerful executive president with impeccable nationalist and military credentials, at first set the military's concerns at rest. But de Gaulle was nothing if not a political realist. He quickly discerned that even if Algeria was a limb of the larger nation, as the imperial *ultras* had long claimed, it had become an infected one and threatened the health of the whole organism. It would simply have to be amputated. Negotiations with the Algerian National Liberation Front rapidly produced an independence agreement which was implemented in 1962.

This was not the end of the story for France. A period of considerable political violence followed as hundreds of thousands of desperate and resentful *pieds noirs* returned to metropolitan France. The more extreme among them came together in the so-called *Organisation de l'Armée Secrète* (OAS) which, through terrorist bombings and plots against de Gaulle's life, sought to reverse the 'betrayal' of Algerian independence. It was a lost cause, of course, and had been from the moment de Gaulle had come to terms with the wider flow of post-war history.

Sub-Saharan Africa

French military reactionaries should not, perhaps, have been completely surprised when de Gaulle sought a negotiated exit from Algeria. His realism about the prospects for French colonialism had already been displayed over the territories of West and Equatorial Africa. Referendums were held throughout the sub-Saharan French empire (including the huge island territory of Madagascar) on de Gaulle's initiative in 1960. These quickly led to a largely smooth and swift process of decolonization. In these territories, of course, there was no significant 'European problem'; they were colonies of exploitation, not of settlement. But the wisdom of France's more graceful exit from this part of its empire was underlined by the network of markedly close post-colonial relationships Paris managed to establish with most of the new states in black Africa which came into being with decolonization. By the mid-1960s France's African possessions were limited to small territories where there were particular obstacles to independence. These included the strategically important Djibouti, located on the coast of the Horn of Africa, and the small island territories of Réunion and Comoros in the Indian Ocean.

The other components of French-speaking Africa – the Belgian Congo along with Rwanda and Burundi (originally German colonies which Belgium had acquired as mandates after the First World War) – became independent between 1960 and 1962. The first of these decolonizations came with immediate disastrous consequences; the others had horrors stored for the future.

Britain led the way in West African decolonization with the independence of Ghana in 1957 under the charismatic prophet of pan-African unity, Kwame Nkrumah. The rest of its West African territories quickly followed, with the regional giant Nigeria becoming independent in 1960. The process was not so smooth elsewhere in British Africa, however. West Africa, with its oppressive climate and spectacular range of tropical diseases, had long been regarded as 'the white man's grave'. It had no

significant European settlement to complicate imperial withdrawal. On the other hand, it did have highly educated and
politically sophisticated local elites ready to take control of the
new states. However, in the east and south of the continent it
was a different picture.

Kwame Nkrumah (1909–1972)

From a Catholic family, in the British colony of the Gold
Coast (Ghana), Nkrumah was educated in church schools and
college before qualifying as a teacher. Temperamentally
unsuited to such an anonymous role, he took the opportunity
to pursue his education with a postgraduate scholarship in the
United States. He returned to the Gold Coast in 1947 as a
confirmed anti-colonial radical by way of Britain where he
spent a period of political activism with other like-minded
young African exiles. Back in Africa he moved easily into a
leadership role in the rapidly growing independence
movement. The Convention People's Party, which he founded,
demanded a rapid British departure and devoted itself to civil
disobedience and industrial action. Although in frequent
trouble with the British colonial administration, Nkrumah's
party dominated the Gold Coast legislature (created in 1951
by the British as a stage towards self-government). With
independence in 1957 he was elected Ghana's first prime
minister. In 1960, after a period of impressive economic
development, Ghana became a republic under his presidency.
On the international stage in the meantime he had become an
eloquent advocate of both pan-Africanism and international
non-alignment. But Ghana's early progress under his rule had
been accompanied by a growing authoritarianism. This
tendency became ever more evident in the 1960s, when it was
no longer balanced by successful economic performance.
Resources were increasingly squandered on grandiose projects
as part of the personality cult that Nkrumah attempted to

build around himself. He was overthrown in an army coup in 1966 while on an official visit to communist China. He died undergoing medical treatment in Romania after a number of years in exile in Guinea.

In Kenya a relatively modest white settler population of about 20,000 provided the focus for a low-level anti-colonial war during the 1950s. The settlers became the target of the Mau-Mau – a politicized secret society dominated by the Kikuyu ethnic group. As in Algeria, the colonial power's response was repression. When reports of the mistreatment of prisoners in detention camps leaked out there was a limited but fierce political reaction in Britain (some of the more shocking details of the suppression of the uprising were still emerging with the declassification of British government papers half a century later). The British had no illusions about remaining indefinitely in Kenya, however. The principle of independence was accepted; the conflict was over the terms on which it would come about. Kenya became an independent state in 1963 under the Kikuyu leader and former political detainee Jomo Kenyatta. Later, Kenyatta became one of the west's firmest friends in Africa and a stalwart of the Commonwealth. This role shift from 'terrorist' to respected statesman in the post-colonial relationship was a familiar feature of the decolonization process.

Jomo Kenyatta (1894?–1978)

Kenyatta was born into the Kikuyu tribe in the Kenyan highlands. At an early age he left the family settlement to attend mission school after which he moved to Nairobi, the British colonial capital. Here, he worked in various clerical posts in the colonial administration. The 1920s saw widespread African protests against the expropriation of land for white settlers, and this movement provided the initial base for Kenyatta's political career. In the years before the Second World War he became well known internationally as he agitated in London for native rights in Kenya and travelled and spoke widely throughout Europe. In the post-war years he was prominent, along with Kwame Nkrumah of Ghana, in the pan-Africanist movement. In 1952 the simmering resentment of the Kikuyu over the alienation of their lands boiled over into anti-settler violence organized by the semi-secret Mau-Mau movement. Kenyatta was arrested and convicted of directing the rebellion (a charge he always denied) and spent nine years in detention. He remained at the head of the anti-colonial movement in Kenya even during this imprisonment, however. He was elected president of the Kenyan African National Union (KANU) while still in prison and the British had no option but to negotiate with him as the pressures for decolonization became irresistible in the early 1960s. Kenyatta became first prime minister of independent Kenya in 1963 and remained in power at the head of a Kikuyu-dominated one-party (KANU) state until his death in 1978. His early radicalism did not long survive independence and under his leadership Kenya became a reliable friend of the west during the cold war.

The situation further south was more complex. This was well illustrated by the ill-conceived British attempt in 1953 to rationalize colonial administration in southern Africa by 'federating' the territories of Northern and Southern Rhodesia and Nyasaland. This forced marriage between different colonies of settlement and exploitation brought the worst of both worlds when African independence appeared on the horizon. Relatively free of European settlement, nationalist activists in Nyasaland and Northern Rhodesia (post-independence Malawi and Zambia respectively) feared the dominance of the white settlers of Southern Rhodesia. These settlers in turn broke away from British colonial rule in 1965 to create a white-controlled state when black rule appeared on the agenda. Not until 1980, after fifteen years of repression and guerrilla war in Africa and political indecision and division in Britain, would Zimbabwe emerge from this as an African-ruled independent state. Even then, the racial conflict engendered by colonialism would bedevil its politics for decades to come.

With the exception of Rhodesia, and the special case of Namibia where UN intervention brought belated independence, both Anglophone and Francophone Africa were substantially decolonized by the mid-1960s. Spain, never a major player in Africa, withdrew from Equatorial Guinea in 1968. It held on to Western Sahara in the north until 1976, however, when it attempted to pass the territory on to its neighbours in northwest Africa – Morocco and Mauritania. The result here was a struggle for self-determination that remained unresolved three decades later.

One sub-Saharan empire remained wholly intact at the beginning of the 1970s: that of Portugal. In the south, the settler colonies of Angola and Mozambique formed part of a mutually supportive white axis along with Apartheid South Africa and rebel Rhodesia. This was fractured in 1974 when a military coup in Lisbon brought a swift end to Portugal's presence in Africa. Portuguese decolonization marked the beginning of the end for white Africa, though the final years would be stained by much blood and destruction. Despite fearful predictions at the time,

Portuguese decolonization marked the beginning of the end for white Africa, though the final years would be stained by much blood and destruction.

however, Portugal itself had a relatively untroubled transition. It managed to absorb its version of the French *pieds noirs* without the violence and instability that France had experienced. Around half a million *retornados*, as they were called, who increased the national population by about 7 per cent, were integrated with remarkable ease into metropolitan Portuguese society after fleeing Angola and Mozambique. The new post-revolutionary, post-colonial Portuguese state then moved quickly into the European economic and diplomatic mainstream of the late twentieth century.

The collapse of the Portuguese empire was widely regarded as the final curtain on the larger colonial drama. Odds and ends of unfinished business remained – in Rhodesia and Namibia, and in the unresolved fate of Western Sahara. Small island territories in the Caribbean and Pacific still clung to the security fence provided by their colonial status as a lesser evil than a struggle for survival in a competitive international system. But this residue could not change the inescapable fact that the colonial era had drawn to a close. Already, however, the first doubts about the nature and totality of that closure were beginning to emerge.

When the tempo of decolonization was at its height in the mid-1960s, almost all of the transfers of power took place in a harmonious and celebratory atmosphere. The prevailing upbeat view in ex-colonies and former imperialist powers alike was that a historical chapter had ended. While it was obvious that the colonial episode would leave a lasting legacy in both the South and

North of the globe, decolonization, it was hoped, had brought a fundamentally new and better world order. United Nations membership (which almost always went with independence) formally affirmed the sovereign equality of the new states, placing them on a diplomatic footing with their one-time masters. The power that the new states could exert on the politics of the UN and in relations between the cold war blocs seemed to be considerable. The global economic environment that the new states entered during the 1960s appeared fundamentally benign. But, over the next decade the practical limitations of post-colonial independence began to reveal themselves. Much of the 'national liberation' that had been fought for and won, often at great cost, began to look more cosmetic than concrete as the harsher realities of post-colonial existence became evident. Hard questions began to press. Had the old colonialism truly been laid to rest – or merely remoulded into a new form?

Decolonization and modernization theory

There was an optimistic script written out for post-colonial development. For a time the ideas of this 'developmentalism', as it was called, dominated progressive thinking in the North and held out the prospect of stability and prosperity for the South. In this scheme formal political independence would open the way for a rapid economic adjustment that would allow the new states to take their place as equal partners in a transformed world economy. The best-known statement of this 'modernization theory' was provided by the American economist W.W. Rostow. In *The Stages of Economic Growth: a Non-Communist Manifesto* published in 1960, he argued that the new countries would undergo a process of accelerated development. Europe and North America had blazed the trail of economic transformation and industrialization in the nineteenth century. The wheel had already been invented, and the blueprint was available for the new players in the international economy. A cohort of entrepreneurs in the former colonies would benefit by not repeating old mistakes and by having tried, tested and successful strategies ready and available. The new countries would therefore achieve rapid 'take-off' into 'modernity'. This would not be exclusively economic; modernization was a complex of interrelated cultural and political dimensions which would bring fundamental social change in the new countries.

It was an interesting and in many ways persuasive theory which chimed with the age's dominant assumptions about the world. These assumptions were liberal, but still fundamentally Eurocentric. The western idea of modernity was the 'right' one and underdeveloped countries should strive to reach it. By the end of the 1960s, however, in large parts of what was now referred to as the Third World, modernization as conceived by Rostow and other developmentalists was simply not happening. Far from rapid take-off into development, large numbers of ex-colonial countries, particularly in sub-Saharan Africa, were becoming more rather than less underdeveloped. A new explanatory theory was needed.

Neocolonialism and dependency theory

This new theory was provided by a group of development economists and political scientists who formulated what came to be known as 'dependency theory'. Writers like Andre Gunder Frank and Samir Amin proposed a model of the post-colonial world quite different from that of the modernization theorists. This alternative perspective was heavily influenced by a neo-Marxist world view. Based initially on studies of Latin America, dependency theory was soon applied to the areas of the world more recently vacated by the European imperial powers. The starting point of dependency theory was that 'underdevelopment' should not be seen as an unfortunate but transitional phase that will be overcome by processes of modernization. On the contrary, underdevelopment was a deliberate policy imposed on the new countries of the South by the dominant countries of the North. Underdevelopment – or 'unequal development' – in the view of dependency theorists was an essential part of the world capitalist system. Successful development in the global South would threaten the economic prosperity of the North because this had been constructed over centuries on the exploitation of the South.

Dependency theory began by re-examining the fundamental economic purposes of colonialism. These, it was argued, provided three essential services to the economy of the imperial power. First, colonialism guaranteed access to controlled markets where goods manufactured in Europe could be sold. Here there was an echo of J.A. Hobson who, at the beginning of the twentieth century, presented imperialism as the outcome of domestic over-production. This over-production could not be absorbed by the impoverished (and therefore under-consuming) workers who actually did the producing and so had to find a market elsewhere. Secondly, colonialism was necessary to capture and exploit sources of raw materials that were either unavailable in Europe or not available in sufficient quantity to meet the needs of metropolitan industry. The murderous acquisition of rubber by King Léopold's agents in the Congo Free State was just one of the more extreme examples of this.

European industry had become dependent on a range of colonial materials, whether tin from Malaya, oil from Arabia or copper from Northern Rhodesia.

European industry had become dependent on a range of colonial materials, whether tin from Malaya, oil from Arabia or copper from Northern Rhodesia. Thirdly, the colonies provided the metropolitan economy with cheap labour. The – often forced – labour of colonial workers was essential if those raw materials were to be extracted and delivered back to the industries of Europe. A cheap labour force was also necessary for the profitable cultivation of cash crops on colonial plantations.

What impact, the dependency theorists asked, would successful development on the model suggested by modernization theory have on this unequal relationship? Quite simply, it would destroy it. 'Development' in the ex-colonial world would spoil everything for the North. Development would mean an end to captive markets for European manufactured goods because the newly developed countries would be producing for their own markets. Development would mean the end of supplies of cheap raw materials because the source country itself would need them for its own industries and any surplus would be traded at prices fixed by world markets. Development would mean the end of a cheap workforce because the labour pool in the former colonies would be drained by new, thriving local economies. It was essential therefore for the North to preserve the basic colonial relationship of dominance and dependency.

The idea of a world divided into two fundamentally unequal but interdependent parts was developed further by a variant of dependency theory. 'World system theory', which is usually associated with the radical economist Immanuel Wallerstein, characterizes this division as one between 'core' (the dominant, developed North) and 'periphery' (the dependent, underdeveloped South). This bipartite world system would, it was claimed, have begun the moment the Spanish conquistadors first set foot in the New World. Henceforward, Europe's economic development rested on a non-European dimension. Development and prosperity for one part of the world was now founded on the underdevelopment and impoverishment of the other. The later growth of tropical empires was designed to formalize this elemental division.

The Marxist element in dependency theory becomes clear if we see this world division between core and periphery as paralleling the class conflict at the centre of Karl Marx's view of capitalism. The core – or capitalist class – sets the terms of the unequal relationship with the periphery – or proletariat. Capitalism can do this because it has been empowered over time by the productivity of the very proletariat that it exploits. The world system parallels this fundamental social and economic relationship. The imperial core grows rich on the exploitation of the colonial periphery. It is essential, of course, that the proletariat remains dependent on the capitalists (or, in global terms, that the periphery remains 'underdeveloped') if the relationship is to go on working as it is designed to do. Fortunately for national capitalism, its economic power allows it to construct the political and cultural framework within which social relationships are conducted. It does so to its own advantage –

just as the 'core' part of the world system sets the rules of international relations.

Yes, but, an obvious line of argument might run, if the maintenance of an unequal colonial relationship is essential to the North's prosperity, why was there wholesale decolonization in the decades after the Second World War? If they were so important to metropolitan well-being it was surely utterly irrational for the imperial powers to rid themselves of their colonies. But no, in the dependency view this was completely rational. In a particular historical era exploitation was maintained most successfully by formal colonial control. But this need not be permanent; times change. A 'colonial' relationship in the broadest sense was certainly necessary, but its political form could vary. It could persist even without the trappings of imperial rule; it could shape-shift into a less formal, but no less exploitative, 'neocolonialism'. At a certain stage the transfer of governmental power, the argument ran, would have no important impact on the relationship of exploitation between colonizer and colonized. Colonial 'independence' amounted to no more than what has been called 'flag decolonization'. The outward symbols of the relationship changed, with different flags being flown on public buildings, but its underlying dynamics remained unaltered. This stage had been reached for most of the colonial powers by the 1960s, according to the dependency theorists.

The mood in the west as much as the east had become hostile to old-fashioned colonialism after 1945. It complicated the pursuit of the cold war and it had become a major source of armed conflict as nationalist movements launched liberation wars. In addition, colonial government had always been expensive. Colonies required administrators, a judicial system and police forces. The colonial state had to provide at least minimal health and education services and was under constant pressure to extend and improve them. Happily for the colonial powers, however, the point at which these pressures began to become unsupportable coincided with the point at which most of these powers were in a position to change the character of colonialism from formal to informal. In other words, they could 'decolonize' because they could simultaneously 'neocolonize'.

A useful image here perhaps is the jelly mould. Formal colonial control, like a glass bowl, 'contains' the fluid economic, political and cultural conditions of the colony. Over time, however, imperial power shapes the colony to its own design. Eventually the shape will hold without the physical constraint of the mould itself which can now be removed. The jelly may wobble a bit afterwards, in extreme cases it may disintegrate, but in general it will hold its shape – a shape determined by the colonial (or, rather, now 'neocolonial') power in its own interests.

What are the processes and mechanisms that 'set the jelly' and allow the mould to be removed? According to dependency theorists, supporting the economic exploitation that is the primary purpose of neocolonialism there is a complex of social, cultural and political forces in place. During the phase of formal imperial control the imperial state will nurture a local elite that will cooperate with the process of exploitation. This has been described as the 'comprador class' (a term borrowed from the local agents used by the Portuguese in Asia in the seventeenth century). This group is co-opted to serve the interests of the colonizer and is rewarded with a privileged position in the colonial state and economy. Its children are educated by the imperial power, usually following the same curriculum taught in Europe (occasionally they will even be *sent* to Europe for this). The lifestyle, indeed the entire world view of this group, will mimic that of the colonizer. In this way a whole section of colonial society becomes separated and alienated from their indigenous culture. They have been indoctrinated into the 'superior' culture of the imperial power. They will become 'little Englishmen', or *'petits français'*.

The most glittering prize awaiting these elites comes with formal independence. They are the recipients of the power transferred from the departing imperial state. Although nominal power may pass to nationalist figureheads, often apparently radical ones, even they will have been formed and educated by the very colonial power they have agitated against. And, critically, their rule will be dependent on the support of a broader political, administrative and professional clique – that comprador class. Post-independence constitutions will mimic those of the metropolis, at least for a time. In former British territories, for example, parliaments will be mini-Westminsters. African lawyers will wilt in the tropical heat under the gowns and wigs inspired by the Old Bailey. New national universities

African lawyers will wilt in the tropical heat under the gowns and wigs inspired by the Old Bailey.

established to produce the next generation of the national elite will be based on those of the old imperial motherland, and will usually be staffed by expatriate academics. The imperial culture thus becomes self-perpetuating despite the absence of imperial rulers. The 'reward' of post-independence power is, of course, primarily a means by which the new ruling elite can continue to serve the old colonial power now in its neocolonial clothes.

Foreign rule by colonial administration is superseded by foreign control by commercial organization. Multinational companies, based in the imperial metropolis but staffed locally by the comprador elite, encounter few difficulties in maintaining the fundamentally unequal economic relationship between imperial power and colony that had existed under the colonial state. These companies can determine labour laws and how they are enforced. They can smother any authentic commercial competition that might threaten to develop. Their control of post-colonial economies in the South is reinforced by the policies of the principal world economic institutions. Throughout the 1980s and 1990s the so-called 'structural adjustment programmes' (SAPs) of the International Monetary Fund imposed the rigours of free-market economics on the weakest states of the South, forcing them into alignment with the prevailing neo-liberal orthodoxies of the North. To their critics in the dependency school these SAPs were designed simply to enforce conformity with the economic preferences of the North, regardless of their social consequences in the South. These consequences led to the further impoverishment of the most vulnerable sections of the population. Previously these parts of society had been protected by at least a minimal level of state intervention and had the possibility of employment in 'unproductive' public sectors. From a Marxist perspective, first the removal of the colonial state and then the enfeeblement of its post-colonial successor simplify the relationship of exploitation. What is any state, after all, but a middle-man between exploiters and exploited?

Clearly, there would be exceptions to the process by which decolonization is followed seamlessly by neocolonization.

Colonies of settlement are problematic in this scheme. Settler communities accustomed to holding the political whip-hand will not give it up lightly, whatever the likelihood of 'true' control remaining with the global North. Rhodesia/Zimbabwe is an obvious example of this, where the white colonial regime rebelled against the decolonizing instincts of the imperial power. Colonies whose primary purpose is strategic rather than economic might not fit the frame either. Britain, uncharacteristically, fought to retain Aden, for example. But even in these cases neocolonial accommodations can be reached, as with the British sovereign bases in post-independence Cyprus or France's continuing military presence in Djibouti. These are exceptions that prove the rule – which was that in the second half of the twentieth century informal control replaced imperial government as the 'colonial' relationship of choice.

At least, it was the choice of those imperial powers in a position to make it. Not all colonizers were able to transform themselves into neocolonialists. Paradoxically, the failure of Spain in the nineteenth century and Portugal in the twentieth to become convincing neocolonialists can be used to 'prove' the larger theory. In Spain's American empire decolonization was more a natural process rather than an 'event'. Yet, the new states that emerged from the process still fell victim to a form of neocolonialism – it was just that the field was opened to other exploiters. Britain and the United States, both much more economically developed than Spain, took on the mantle Spain was unable to wear. Significantly, both of these powers had worked to speed Spain's departure from the Americas by actively supporting nationalist forces. The tendency towards a 'world system' of dominant core and exploited periphery, in other words, cannot be resisted.

Why was Portugal so determined, apparently to the point of obsession, to stay in Africa when the other European powers had slipped away? Why did it insist on hanging on by its fingernails in the face of guerrilla wars across its empire? What rational reason was there for a poor and weak country on the edge of Europe to cling on to a huge empire against the strictures of the world? There are *irrational* explanations, certainly. One is that Portugal was in the grip of a national delusion. Its authoritarian conservative leaders may really have believed that the country formed the spiritual heart of a vast, unified 'pluricontinental' phenomenon. However, along with this, perhaps, was a more logical calculation. Portugal may have bound itself to empire not *in spite* of its own weakness but *because* of it. Itself an underdeveloped country displaying the characteristics of a dependent periphery within Europe, Portugal could not decolonize because, quite simply, it could not neocolonize. Once its formal and highly protectionist grip was removed from Angola and Mozambique, Portugal would be marginalized there by stronger economic powers. In the same way that Latin America became 'neocolonized' by Britain and the United States in the nineteenth century, southern Africa would be plucked from Portugal by the power of foreign multinational companies. If Portugal was to wring any economic benefit from Africa, therefore, it had no choice but to defy the larger march of history by holding on to its formal empire. History not readily being defied, of course, the outcome was revolution in Portugal and the rapid disintegration of the empire.

Challenges to dependency theory

Dependency theory is seductive on several fronts. It is an elegant theory in many ways, very satisfying in the neat interconnections it seems to establish between different political, economic and cultural phenomena. It has a convincing intellectual architecture. It also provides an explanation for the failure of development in the post-colonial world that did not 'blame the victim'. The opportunity it offers to denounce international capitalism as the villain of the piece was particularly welcome on the political left. Western liberals and socialists had been put on the back foot by the manifest shortcomings of leaders and movements they had championed in the anti-colonial struggle. Perhaps it was not their fault after all. To focus on internal failings in the underdeveloped countries themselves, in fact, could come uncomfortably close to racism. It was no coincidence that the intellectual milieu in the west in the late 1960s and 1970s, when interest in dependency theory was at its height, was dominated by the anti-racist left. But the theory has real weaknesses and can be criticized from a number of directions.

One of the most powerful arguments against the dependency perspective is its excessive 'reductionism'. By definition, of course, all theory is reductionist; that is its *raison d'être*. Its purpose is to boil down different data into a central explanatory model. But the broad and simple division of the world into a political-economic core and periphery seems to fly in the face of the evidence and common sense. Yes, Niger might lie firmly in the periphery and France in the core. There would be no argument either about placing Honduras and the United States in this scheme. However, most country-by-country judgements are less clear. What about the so-called 'Asian tigers', for example? Malaysia, Singapore and Indonesia are all former European colonies, but their post-colonial position in the world economy would seem to support Rostow's modernization theory rather than the dependency model. All of them underwent a process of accelerated development after independence and all have become significant economic actors in their own right. More strikingly, India is frequently hailed as an emerging economic superpower for the twenty-first century, a status it is apparently moving towards on the basis of its own national drive.

The enormously varying fortunes of different former colonies suggest that a greater focus on internal social, economic and political conditions is required. On one hand, this might seem to carry a danger of cultural stereotyping. But

The enormously varying fortunes of different former colonies suggest that a greater focus on internal social, economic and political conditions is required.

on the other, to impose a single monolithic identity on the greater part of the world is itself a form of cultural insensitivity. There is simply no escaping the fact that the experience of former colonies in Asia is generally different from that of former colonies in sub-Saharan Africa. To be fair, some elaborations of dependency theory have attempted to meet such objections. Wallerstein, for example, developed the idea of a 'semi-periphery' to ease the rigidity of the basic division. But the accusation of over-simplification remains valid.

The insistence that there is a world system comparable to class relations in capitalist countries has drawn criticism from within the left itself. Writers in the classical Marxist tradition like Bill Warren insist that there is no such thing as a 'global division of labour'. Basing his case on a close study of India's colonial and post-colonial economy, Warren argued (long before India's current surge of economic energy) that national capitalism develops naturally within all states. In the Marxist view, after all, states *exist* to serve the well-being of capitalism. Capitalist development will take place at a different pace from country to country depending on local circumstances, but it will always take place. Interestingly, Warren (and indeed Karl Marx himself) was very close to the modernization theorists in this view. Rostow and his supporters saw the development of national capitalism in the former colonies as the final destination, while the Marxist purists considered it as a stage in the march towards world communism. Both, however, regarded capitalism as a 'progressive' colonial export rather than a mechanism for the perpetual exploitation of the South by the North.

During the 1980s dependency theory rather went out of vogue. This was due in part to its inability to accommodate the type of objections just raised. But more generally it also suffered from the growing influence of postmodernist thinking, with its rejection of single grand theories. Dependency theory was nothing if not an over-arching 'meta-narrative'. As a result, the failure of development, particularly in Africa, was increasingly explained with reference to local conditions. Rather than blaming underdevelopment on neocolonialism, theorists of 'neo-patrimonialism' argued that it was a consequence of the re-appearance of pre-colonial cultural and political relationships. In this view, the elites who inherited the post-colonial state did not in fact behave as the obedient 'compradors' of dependency theory. Having acquired control of the new country they scraped off the veneer of Europeanism applied by their colonial masters and reasserted their native identity. These elites were drawn to highly personalized political forms based on a patron–client relationship. This type of politics was similar to that which had existed before the arrival of the European colonizers. The 'neo-patrimonial' theorists argued that this created an impossible obstacle to (western-style) development. These re-emerging, pre-colonial forms of politics were fundamentally incompatible with modern production and commerce and could not accommodate the political structures that were necessary for successful capitalism to flourish.

Dependency theory suffered other blows in the 1990s. One came with the end of the cold war. In reality, the collapse of the Soviet Union had little to do with the failure of 'socialism' in any meaningful sense, but it still had an impact on intellectual debate. Marxism in all its forms – including that of dependency theory – was put on the defensive. Later, though, with the rising awareness of the speed and extent of globalization at the turn of the twenty-first century, the dependency perspective (or at least some of its propositions) enjoyed a bit of a renaissance. Debates about what the process of globalization is actually all about can come close to validating a dependency view of the world. The optimistic view of globalization represents it as a universalization of cultures and economies. In this new order all countries make a contribution to the creation of an interconnected global community. Against this, however, is a view of globalization as a process of westernization. The developed world, in other words, can project its economic and political power to shape the rest of the globe to its advantage and in its preferred image. This perspective was neatly summed up by Martin Khor, the Malaysian economist, in an address to the International Forum on Globalization in 1995. 'Globalization', he observed, 'is what we in the Third World have for several centuries called colonization.'

Recommended reading

The generalities of European decolonization are dealt with by Franz Ansprenger in *The Dissolution of the Colonial Empires* (London: Routledge, 1987) and R.F. Holland in *European Decolonization, 1918–81* (London: Macmillan, 1985). Muriel E. Chamberlain's *Longman Companion to European Decolonization in the Twentieth Century* (London: Longman, 1998) provides a useful systematic account of the process.

British policy and the range of interpretations given to it are explored in John Darwin's *The End of the British Empire: The Historical Debate* (Oxford: Blackwell, 1991). France's fraught departures from Vietnam and Algeria are the subject of Anthony Clayton's *The Wars of French Decolonization* (London: Longman, 1994), while its less violent withdrawal from sub-Saharan Africa is dealt with by Tony Chafer in *The End of Empire in French West Africa* (Oxford: Berg, 2002). Portugal's rapid exit from Africa is explored by Norrie MacQueen in *The Decolonization of Portuguese Africa: Metropolitan Revolution and the Dissolution of Empire* (London: Longman, 1997).

Walt Rostow's key text on modernization theory is still in print: *The Stages of Economic Growth: A Non Communist Manifesto* (Cambridge: Cambridge University Press, 1991). The seminal works of the dependency theorists are not the most accessible way into their work. However, Andre Gunder Frank and Barry Gills: *The World System: Five Hundred Years or Five Thousand* (London: Taylor & Francis, 1993) and *The Essential Wallerstein* (New York: New Press, 2001) provide more user-friendly introductions. Ian Roxborough's *Theories of Underdevelopment* (London: Macmillan, 1979) gives a concise overview of the different models of post-colonial underdevelopment. Dependency theory is attacked from an orthodox Marxist stance by Bill Warren (his book's title a play on that of Lenin's 1916 tract) in *Imperialism: Pioneer of Capitalism* (London: Verso, 1980).

CHAPTER 7

The many faces of post-colonialism

THE WORLD OF THE TWENTY-FIRST CENTURY is, inescapably, a product of colonialism. One does not have to subscribe to the idea of a 'world system' built on neocolonialism, or the division of the world into a dominant core and a dependent periphery, to acknowledge this. It is a truth that is evident at just about every level of human experience in both North and South.

Colonialism and its aftermath have determined the whole character of contemporary international relations. At the most basic level, colonialism laid the foundations for an international system constructed from the fundamental building blocks of independent territorial states. Beyond this, old colonial relationships have had a powerful influence on the contemporary foreign policies of former imperialists and former subject nations alike, for good and bad. Old affinities have evolved into modern diplomatic loyalties and have produced a range of post-colonial institutions. On the dark side, colonialism lies somewhere below the surface of most of the violent conflicts that afflict the contemporary world, whether between North and South or among states of the South, or within them. The so-called 'war on terror' – in the Middle East, Asia and Africa – is perhaps not the Manichean struggle between good and evil, darkness and light that its more enthusiastic supporters claim. Its roots lie in the complex of unresolved problems over land, culture and perceived inequalities in the distribution of world power that is a heritage of colonialism. At a less apocalyptic level but a no less lethal one, regional and civil conflicts, from central and West Africa to south Asia and on to the islands of the South Pacific, have grown directly out of the colonial history of these regions.

The impact of colonialism goes further and deeper than international politics. Over the past centuries the globe has undergone a linguistic revolution. The language map of

> *Over the past centuries the globe has undergone a linguistic revolution.*

the contemporary world has the same broad colours as the markings on the old ones showing the extent of the European empires. Spanish, French, Portuguese and, above all, English are the linguas francas of the planet in the twenty-first century. Everything from eating habits to national sports and entertainments have been shaped and altered by the colonial experience, and this process has operated in both directions.

In working towards some kind of assessment of the enduring impact of colonialism in the twenty-first century we have to explore these legacies. How and with what success have formal political relations persisted between the former 'sides' in the colonial relationship? At a deeper social and cultural level, what constitutes the intellectual idea of 'post-colonialism'? And, what are we really witnessing in the North's increasingly frequent involvement in the conflicts of the South? Is this 'humanitarian intervention' driven by altruism or by post-colonial guilt? Or is it something else – a shouldering of the 'white man's burden' once again in a renewed attempt to re-shape the world in the North's image and interests after the failure of the previous ones? In short, are we in an age of 're-colonization'?

Persisting political and security relationships

The Commonwealth, *La Francophonie* and the Community of Portuguese-Speaking Countries (*Comunidade dos Países de Língua Portuguesa*: CPLP) are each in their different ways a residue of distinctive national approaches to empire and colonialism by Britain, France and Portugal respectively. Each illustrates the persistence of attitudes and ideas forged amidst the old certainties of imperial Europe, their adaptability to new circumstances and their capacity to make an impact on contemporary international relations.

Among the three movements this is perhaps most evident in the Commonwealth. The old British Commonwealth, which originally tied the white dominions of South Africa, Canada, Australia and New Zealand to the mother country, evolved quietly and pragmatically. Dropping the 'British' in the 1960s and acquiring a permanent headquarters and secretariat, it absorbed virtually every one of the newly independent states that appeared after decolonization. The rules and requirements of membership remain minimal. Although its headquarters are located in London it is a highly decentralized institution with no one member or group of members dominating its political agenda. The obvious complaint against all this is that the

Commonwealth's pragmatism and the minimal requirements it imposes on members make it a fundamentally weak, even irrelevant political institution. However this may be, the relationship between the institution and British imperial philosophy at the beginning of the twentieth century seems clear. The ghost of Frederick Lugard would probably have little difficulty in understanding its institutional dynamics.

The Commonwealth manages more or less successfully to bind together some fifty-three states populated by about three billion people in total, some 30 per cent of the world's population. The necessary price for this reach, however, is a corresponding lack of depth in the requirements and obligations of membership. The Commonwealth operates without a formal constitution on the basis of a kind of pragmatic minimalism. Yet it is striking that transition from imperial possession to Commonwealth member was virtually automatic and universal throughout the British empire. Only Burma and Sudan chose not to seek membership and others who from time to time have withdrawn or been suspended have invariably returned.

The Commonwealth manages more or less successfully to bind together some fifty-three states populated by about three billion people in total

By an odd coincidence *La Francophonie* also has fifty-three members, but that is about the only point of comparison with the Commonwealth. *La Francophonie* is less a formal post-colonial institution than a cultural association with political undertones. Five of its members (Belgium, Bulgaria, Luxembourg, Monaco and Switzerland) and several other associate members and observers are European states. The French-speaking Canadian provinces are members, as are some former colonies of Portugal and Belgium. It is, in short, an institution of a former imperial state determined to assert the continuing importance of its cultural and political heritage. To this extent the roots of *La Francophonie* can be located in the same philosophical and political soil as those of France's colonial practices. The Enlightenment and the French Revolution have shaped both. The absences from *La Francophonie* are telling, though. Several of France's most important former colonies, including Algeria and Guinea, have declined to participate, leaving *La Francophonie* in a situation roughly analogous to a Commonwealth without India and Nigeria. The well of post-colonial resentment, at least in parts of the Francophone world, runs deep.

The Portuguese organization, the CPLP, includes all of the former colonies, but their commitment and enthusiasm are far from uniform. On a number of occasions since its formation in 1996 the CPLP has seemed more or less moribund. Portugal is a relative newcomer to post-colonial diplomacy for the obvious reason that its colonialism lasted longest. Its attempts at institution-building have generally been less successful than those of Britain and France. But it is not just the time factor of Portugal's belated decolonization process that has affected its post-colonial relationships. Portugal's expulsion from its colonies was sudden and unprepared for. It came as the culmination of long and bitter wars. The necessary bases for either a sentimental, evolutionary Commonwealth or a culturally assertive *Francophonie* simply did not exist.

The CPLP emerged after a number of false starts more than twenty years after Portugal's last colonies became independent.

Its members included, crucially for its institutional credibility, Brazil, the largest of the world's Portuguese-speaking countries. In terms of membership, therefore, the CPLP, like *La Francophonie* (or the Commonwealth if the United States were a member), is a post-colonial organization only in the broadest sense. Enthusiasm for the CPLP has always been greatest in Portugal itself – sometimes rather ruefully so. The attitudes of the other members illustrate the peculiar dilemma of Portugal's post-imperial status and look back to its particular colonial obsessions. Brazil's attention seemed to wander after initial interest. Mozambique was always a wary participant. It has given much greater importance to its membership of the Commonwealth (which it was permitted to join because of its peculiar geopolitical location in Anglophone southern Africa). The hard reality in this for Portugal is that Commonwealth membership carries diplomatic and material benefits far greater than those offered by the CPLP.

This encapsulates Portugal's difficulty. Possession of vast colonies had defined it as a significant international entity. Without them its diplomatic and economic weakness became clear. Membership of the CPLP therefore is rather less than a political and economic 'must-have' for its former colonies. Its one appeal lies in the exclusivity of the Portuguese language and the services it can provide to help poor countries work in the medium. Language was the one distinctive 'gift' of Portuguese culture. Imposed on the empire with centralized rigidity, it remains the one substantial strand tying Portugal to its former colonies.

These formal post-colonial institutions cover only part of the spectrum of contemporary relationships between the components of the old empires. Overall, it has not been a particularly important part. Among them only the Commonwealth has played a truly significant role in serious post-colonial diplomacy. It was, for example, a key actor in Rhodesia's transition from minority white rule to African statehood as Zimbabwe in 1979 and 1980. The interventions of the Commonwealth have also had an impact in the internal politics of independent states. It was a major source of pressure on Apartheid South Africa and operated a regime of economic sanctions against the government there until the 1990s. It has also had a role in maintaining at least a form of democracy in Fiji when inter-communal tensions between indigenous Melanesians and the country's ethnic Indian population threatened the political process at various times. More typical of the fate of such post-colonial interventions, however, was the CPLP's experience in the late 1990s when it attempted to resolve the civil war in Guinea-Bissau. The alliance quickly unravelled, exposing the venture as primarily a Portuguese project rather than a truly multilateral one.

The most significant post-colonial connections are to be found, paradoxically, not in the institutions dedicated to them but in other international organizations. The European Union embraces all of the former colonial powers of Europe and manages a vast system of continuing engagement with the former colonies through its various ACP (Africa, Caribbean, Pacific) programmes. The European Development Fund is perhaps the most important multilateral aid source outside the United Nations system and, although not exclusively concerned with EU members' former territories, certainly favours them. It represents a halfway-house between traditional bilateral aid arrangements and an increasing tendency towards multilateralism in the distribution and management of development assistance.

The place of the former colonies in the larger project of European integration was acknowledged right from the initial signing of the Treaty of Rome in 1957 when the European Economic Community (as it was then called) was first created. The so-called Yaoundé agreements (named for the capital of Cameroon where they were signed) of 1963 and 1969 established preferential economic and political relations between the Community and the ex-colonies of founder members (France, Belgium and Holland). When Britain joined the European project in 1973, a new arrangement was signed in Lomé, the Togolese capital, which with successive revisions carried on into the new millennium, absorbing additional territories following the admission of Portugal and Spain. The Lomé conventions – and a subsequent agreement signed in yet another West African capital, Cotonou in Benin – have played a very important role in cushioning post-colonial trade relations against the worst of the free-market consequences of European integration. Their impact on larger issues of inequalities in world trade has been scant, however.

Despite the shift towards managing relations with former colonies through international organizations, old-fashioned one-to-one links remain important. France in particular has established a network of close economic

Despite the shift towards managing relations with former colonies through international organizations, old-fashioned one-to-one links remain important.

and security relationships with Africa. The 'West African franc' is one of the most stable currencies in sub-Saharan Africa. It binds together not just the former French territories but adjacent countries as well (Portugal was severely put out when Guinea-Bissau opted to enter the franc zone in order to align its economy more closely with its large French-speaking neighbours, Senegal and Guinea).

For better or for worse, French troops have been engaged in a range of political and security crises throughout France's former colonies in Africa in the 1990s and 2000s. Foreign Legion and other forces have seen action in Chad, the Central African Republic and Côte d'Ivoire. Even more controversially, a French force was deployed in Rwanda at the end of the 1994 genocide. Here, according to the Tutsi-dominated forces poised to seize power, the real objective of the French intervention was to aid the escape of their erstwhile allies, the Hutu extremists who had orchestrated the slaughter. Britain, perhaps more wary of accusations of neocolonialism than France, has been less directly engaged with security problems in its former territories. It tried, for example, to deal with the chaos inflicted on Zimbabwe under the despotic rule of Robert Mugabe through the Commonwealth rather than by unilateral intervention. Perhaps predictably, the range of incompatible interests that lie at the heart of the internal politics of the Commonwealth doomed this approach to failure. However, British paratroops and Special Air Service forces were crucial in preserving the weak and unstable but democratic government of Sierra Leone against a brutal warlord insurgency in 2000 and 2001.

Elsewhere, in situations where there has been military intervention by the United Nations in former colonial territories, the ex-imperial powers have frequently had a special – and occasionally controversial – role. Britain formed a major part of the UN operation in Cyprus after 1964 (largely because of the presence of available troops in the sovereign base areas and their familiarity with the terrain). The French have played an important role in UN forces in Lebanon, as have the Italians in Somalia. Belgian UN troops bore the brunt of the initial violence during the Rwanda genocide, and Portuguese forces have been deployed in international forces in Angola, Mozambique and later East Timor. In almost all of these crises in the post-colonial world, questions were asked about whether, if push came to shove, the loyalty of the contingents from the old imperial powers would be to the UN chain of command or to the neocolonial instincts of former rulers.

'Humanitarian intervention' or 'liberal imperialism'?

This matter of post-colonial military involvement raises an issue that goes wider than particular relationships between ex-colonies and their former masters. In many parts of the world decolonization abruptly ended local security arrangements previously provided by the colonial power. Often, the removal of this 'imperial order' made no real difference, as the new states proved perfectly capable of managing their own security. In other, less stable regions, the old imperial power retained a security role (like the French in West Africa, for example). Elsewhere the imperial order of the European colonialists was quickly replaced by a new version imposed by the leaders of the cold war blocs. In parts of Africa, the Middle East and particularly Asia the superpowers established spheres of influence on the departure of the European imperialists. These helped maintain a degree of regional peace and security, especially during periods when the relationship between those superpowers was less tense and their respective spheres of interest were mutually respected. But the end of the cold war, although obviously a 'good thing' in its larger effect on the international system, removed this second imperial order from the former colonial world. The great surge in conflict management by the UN and other international actors in the 1990s was only in part a positive development in international relations; to an extent it was a necessary response to increased disorder.

The security vacuum created by the end of the cold war has been filled by UN peacekeepers, so-called 'coalitions of the willing', or on occasion by former colonial powers acting alone. A new political and military lexicon has developed to describe this activity, the key term of which is 'humanitarian intervention'. For the optimist this is a fundamental advance in international relations, nothing less than a shift towards a form of 'global governance'. This position is described by political theorists as 'cosmopolitanism' (meaning literally 'universal polity'). Its advocates see the international system slowly but surely turning into a genuine international 'community'. Cosmopolitanism assumes the existence of a set of basic values shared by all humanity. Powers equipped for the task should therefore accept a responsibility to nurture and defend these norms everywhere in the community. As a fundamentally liberal world view, cosmopolitanism places democracy and human rights at the centre of this global value system.

From the cosmopolitanist perspective the end of the cold war simplified relations between North and South. The North no longer viewed its relations with the former colonial world through the prism of the east–west competition. Repressive anti-democratic regimes in Africa, Asia and Latin America need no longer be supported by the west, as they had been in the past, as 'bulwarks against communism'. In parallel with this, the promises held out by equally undemocratic communist routes to development lost almost all credibility in the South. The more or less total collapse of the Soviet bloc exposed the hollowness of such schemes with the disappearance of the part of the international system that had advocated them. Now, the process of globalization could potentially provide a powerful vehicle by which the new international community could sow and nurture the seeds of universal liberal norms. Humanitarian intervention by military forces represents the 'sharp end' of this project, a practical expression of responsibility to the new communal world order.

So far, so progressive, but questions begin to gather. Is there in truth an identifiable set of unvarying human values

Is there in truth an identifiable set of unvarying human values and associated rights?

and associated rights? Or do different cultures, religions and ethnicities evolve their own values, which may be quite distinct from those in other parts of the world? There may be *dominant* standards and norms in the world, but are they in reality *universal*? If they are dominant, how have they become so? Could it be that the dominance of these values has to do with the relative power in the world of the countries that hold them? If they are not universal, why are they being represented as such? Could it be that the efforts to implant them are simply a new version of the 'civilizing mission'? Are we witnessing not humanitarian intervention to uphold indivisible human values but a form of 'liberal imperialism' designed to enforce their adoption? In other words, is this merely the 'white man's burden' *de nos jours?* Backlit in this way the whole humanitarian project, constructed and pursued by the global North (whether wearing the blue beret of the United Nations or not), can begin to seem less progressive and more, as we might say, *colonialist.*

The argument could be taken further. Not only is this interventionism misguided; it may not even be altruistic. Just as the rhetoric of the white man's burden at the turn of the twentieth century disguised all sorts of ruthless self-interest on the part of the colonialists, so perhaps at the turn of the twenty-first does talk of humanitarian intervention. This proposition gained force after the terrorist attacks in the United States in 2001. The ensuing 'war on terror' is aimed in part to bolster fundamentally 'western' political cultures where they are thought to be threatened and to impose them where they do not exist. The American-led invasions of Afghanistan and Iraq are the most obvious examples of this. In this way, genuinely progressive strategies designed to nurture the development of a world community can lie uncomfortably close to the neo-conservative project. This neo-conservatism does not exist primarily to spread liberal values throughout the world but to remove perceived threats to the west by crushing all but western norms. Cynics have suggested the slogan 'live free or die' for the neo-conservative approach to 'choice' in the world.

There is another dimension to this self-interest which is less to do with forms of government than with the basic structure within which governments relate to each other. The contemporary international system is often described as 'Westphalian'. Having emerged in seventeenth-century Europe after the Thirty

Years War (which ended with the Treaty of Westphalia), this system is based on the principle of sovereign equality between territorial states. Each and every inch of the planet is, supposedly, part of a particular state. Each of these states conducts relations with other states on the basis of absolute independence. In legal if not in cultural and political terms, the empires of the nineteenth and twentieth centuries were extensions of the European states which ruled over them. Decolonization created new sovereignties and each of these had its own physical borders with neighbouring sovereignties. It was unthinkable that any other arrangement could exist. The territorial state was the fundamental building block of the system, and any gaps in the brickwork would threaten the stability of the whole edifice. States knew the rules of the game and were

The territorial state was the fundamental building block of the system, and any gaps in the brickwork would threaten the stability of the whole edifice.

accountable to the Westphalian collective for their behaviour. This may not have amounted to an international 'community', but it was a rudimentary international 'society'. It imposed a limited order on what might otherwise be global anarchy. Conveniently, the new national elites to whom power was transferred after independence were more than happy to work within the Westphalian model. It was well suited to the mobilization of European-style nationalism. This could be exploited to advance the post-colonial nation-building project or be manipulated to selfish ends, depending on the good or ill intentions of leaders.

In some of the new states this arrangement worked well. It was ideally suited to former colonies of settlement where a largely European political class retained power after independence (for example, in the Americas and in Britain's white dominions). It also worked reasonably well in most of Asia where the territorial organization of power was familiar long before any colonial incursion from Europe. In other parts, however, particularly Africa, where the type of patrimonial culture we described in the last chapter was common and where clear geographical divisions between 'nations' were rare, the territorial state soon came under pressure. In extreme cases this led to the collapse of the state as a workable political entity. The system responded initially by in effect pretending this was not happening. The phenomenon of 'quasi-states', described by the Canadian political scientist Robert Jackson, emerged. These were to be found from sub-Saharan Africa to the South Pacific. Although they had the outward trappings of Westphalian 'units' and were treated as such by the rest of the system, in reality these countries were virtually stateless territories.

Somalia provides a revealing example of the phenomenon. Decolonized in 1960 after the unification of the Italian and British territories in the region, its highly clan-based, patrimonial political culture soon began to reassert itself. Initially, its position on the periphery of the system meant that it could be treated as a quasi-state without raising too many concerns. By the 1970s, however, the whole of the Horn of Africa had become an area of intense cold war competition. The imposition of imperial order, which had ended with decolonization, was now replaced by order imposed by the superpowers. The end of the cold war then removed any urgent reason for outsiders to maintain stability. The United States now effectively abandoned its 'client', the dictatorial President Siyaad Barre, and the Somali state disintegrated amidst fighting between rival warlords. The efforts of a joint United Nations–United States 'humanitarian intervention' in the early 1990s failed, and Somalia was once again left as a stateless entity, a missing brick in the Westphalian wall. This was just about tolerable as long as Somalia remained on the periphery of international relations and posed no threat to the interests of the big powers. With the declaration of the war on terror, however, western (particularly American) interest in Somalia suddenly revived. Any entity lying outside the boundaries of the Westphalian system had now become a potential threat. And, when it was an Islamic entity like Somalia, the threat was seen as a critical one.

From this sequence of events it is possible to see the twenty-first century ideas of democratic 'norm transfer' and humanitarian intervention entwined with the older ones of colonial domination. Colonialism left not just western models of government in the ex-colonial world; the new states were tied into a particular form of global relationship. The contemporary world in this very concrete way therefore was 'constructed' by colonialism. The main interests served by this colonial legacy are those of the former colonialists. For the North the universal implantation of western values and the integrity of the Westphalian system in the twenty-first century are not simply goods bestowed on the world but instruments of self-preservation. The 'black man's burden', in effect.

In reality, of course, the tension between humanitarian intervention and 're-colonization' is not as great as this account might suggest. If humanitarian intervention has a dark side within which all sorts of ulterior motives lurk, it is also in most cases a genuine expression of human concern and altruism. It is often a policy forced on wary governments in the North by well-intentioned public pressure. A century or more before, colonial ventures were begun reluctantly by governments at the urgings of philanthropists concerned at the abject state of the 'dark-skinned races'. But while in the earlier period the sources for such pressure were missionary reports, contemporary consciences are pricked by the 'CNN-effect', instant and graphic news reports from all parts of the world. The nineteenth-century liberal imperialist thought consciously about a 'white man's burden'; his contemporary equivalent is driven by a less articulate humanitarianism. Whether it amounts to the same thing – a colonialist reflex – depends very much on the political perspective of the observer. At the level of government policy making the picture is even more difficult to bring into focus. Intervention will often be reluctantly undertaken, as in Rwanda during the genocide of 1994, for example. However, self-interest will always be present, as in the attempt to impose a change of regime in Afghanistan after the terrorist attacks in 2001, for instance. The only safe pronouncement in this contested area is that re-colonization in a direct and literal sense is not an option any western government will contemplate at the beginning of the twenty-first century. The discourse of self-determination is now universal. It may be navigated around in several ways, but it will rarely be directly challenged.

Post-colonialism, culture and society

The colonial episode has of course left a cultural and social legacy that goes much further than high politics and international relations. Day-to-day life in the greater part of the planet is coloured in all kinds of way by the experience of colon-ization. The impact on those in once-colonizing nations is frequently as marked as that on the once-colonized. 'Post-colonialism', one of the most significant intellectual movements of the late twentieth century, has been concerned with this reality.

'Post-colonial theory', as it is sometimes called, rejects the once dominant 'Eurocentric' narrative of colonialism and its aftermath. Approaches to the study of colonialism and its impact, post-colonialists argue, have conventionally been those of the imperialist. They have reflected the preoccupations of the colon-izer rather than those of the colonized. As a result, a whole dimension of world history and culture has been marginalized. Even the strongest historical voices of anti-colonialism, like those of Lenin and Hobson, came from an essentially imperialist per-spective. Their analyses focused on the economic mechanisms of colonialism in Europe rather than its impact on the lives of the colonized. A similar situation existed with literary accounts of imperialism. While Joseph Conrad was an eloquent critic of the inhumanity of European colonialism, he persisted in representing Africa itself as a separated, unknowable 'heart of darkness' rather than as simply an innocent victim of foreign greed and brutality.

In order to fully understand the significance of colonialism to the contemporary world, post-colonial theorists argue, a more comprehensive perspective is required. The emphasis has to be shifted towards the colonized and away from the colonizer whose 'hegemonic' authority has in the past dictated what was studied, how and with what conclusions. To this end, post-colonialism ('poco' to those in the 'business') champions historical interpret-ations, social studies and literary representations that focus on the experience of the colonized – or, to use the theoretical term, the 'subaltern': those subordinated to the hegemony of the colonizer.

In some respects, of course, this approach to the analysis of colonialism is not new. Colonial intellectuals like Frantz Fanon and Gandhi had already offered what were in essence post-colonial explorations of French and British imperialism during the colonial period itself. However, post-colonial theory, as normally understood, emerged more recently. Its beginnings are usually linked with the work of the United States-based Palestinian writer, Edward Said. In his influential book *Orientalism*, published in 1978, Said explored the western construction of colonial 'otherness'. The imperial sense of superiority, he argued, was grounded in the presentation of foreign cultures and peoples as fundamentally different from – and inferior to – those of the imperial power. These representations dealt in carefully manufactured stereotypes which could be placed in direct opposition to the supposed virtues of the west. The emotionalism of the alien races was contrasted with the rationality of the westerner. Oriental decadence was pitched against the industriousness of the European. The capricious power of the oriental despot was compared unfavourably with the rule of law imposed by the imperial power. The idea of a 'white man's burden', according to Said, was self-created and self-serving and built on a series of convenient caricatures. While Said's work dealt primarily with western attitudes to the Islamic world, its broader relevance to the colonial experience was clear. Colonization had been justified on the basis of manufactured differences; a massive moral deceit lay at its heart.

Edward Said (1935–2003)

A Palestinian Christian born in Jerusalem, Said became one of America's leading public intellectuals of the second half of the twentieth century. As an academic literary critic (he spent most of his working life at Columbia University), he was particularly interested in western fictional characterizations of non-Europeans and the social and political factors that lay behind these. Much of his early work in this area was concerned with the writings of Joseph Conrad. The book with which his name is most closely associated, however, is *Orientalism*, which he published in 1978. In this, Said anatomized western views of the Islamic and Asiatic worlds. These perceptions, he argued, cast the 'oriental' in the role of unknowable 'other' lying beyond the frontiers of western 'civilization'. This carefully crafted image, he suggested, provided an excuse for colonization and a justification for colonialism. A similar theme was pursued in his book *Culture and Imperialism* (1993). He gave a more personal slant to the cultural divide between east and west in his autobiography, *Out of Place*, published in 1999. Said was a tireless advocate of Palestinian rights, though he insisted that a viable Palestinian state could only be created through dialogue. An accomplished musician, he cooperated with the Israeli pianist and conductor Daniel Barenboim in ventures bringing young Palestinians and Israelis together through musical performance.

Language and diaspora

When surveying the enduring social and cultural consequences of colonialism it can be difficult to separate effects (in both the North and the South) that come directly out of the colonial relationship from changes that are due simply to increased human mobility and communication. This is particularly the case with language. There can be no question that colonialism has had a deep and long-term impact on contemporary linguistic patterns in the world. This is not a modern phenomenon. The major languages of south-western Europe – French, Spanish and Portuguese among them – are Latin based. Their origins lie in the projection of the imperial power of Rome in past millennia. Today, more than one-and-a-quarter billion people in the world routinely use either one of these three languages or English (which has its own Germanic 'colonial' origins). They do so as a result of the latest wave of linguistic colonialism dating mainly from the eighteenth and nineteenth centuries. The combined population of the four European countries themselves (about 172 million) accounts for only a tiny fraction of the total world use of 'their' languages.

Sub-Saharan African regions are frequently defined as Anglophone, Francophone or Lusophone, categories that have political and cultural dimensions going far beyond the confines of language use. There has been no wholesale reversion to traditional language use in Africa since decolonization. Part of this obviously has to do with elite perceptions of 'modernization' and the manufactured disdain for indigenous culture of the westernized 'comprador' class. However, retention of the colonial language in Africa has had practical purposes in post-independence states as well.

Language	Metropolitan Use	World Use
English	60.6 million	510 million
Spanish	40.4 million	425 million
Portuguese	10.6 million	218 million
French	60.9 million	130 million

The systematic suppression of local languages was a component part of Portugal's rigidly centralized colonial rule. Language was central to the mythology of luso-tropicalism. However, after independence the radical Marxist regimes in

> *Language was central to the mythology of luso-tropicalism.*

Mozambique, Angola and Guinea-Bissau proved just as determined to retain Portuguese as their national language. There were two important reasons for this. First, a single, universally spoken language had huge practical value as a vehicle for administration, education and political propaganda. Secondly, a single language could have an important unifying effect in states whose very existence was threatened by regionalism and tribalism. Any attempt to select one local language and impose its use would be counter-productive and would provoke even greater division. The limited use of Swahili as a national language in Tanzania and Kenya was possible because it was not identified with a particular ethnicity (in fact, Swahili with its many Arabic influences could itself be called a 'colonial' language). The Portuguese language therefore had a role in African nation-building – a use that could not have been further from the intentions of those who first imposed it on Africa. Anecdote now has it that in Mozambique, where the English of the surrounding countries is making inroads, Portuguese is now a badge of nationalism for a new generation of young intellectuals and activists. The old colonial language here seems to have become a defence against the new colonialism of globalization.

The processes of cultural exchange most certainly did not travel in only one direction. Colonialism has had profound social effects on the post-imperial countries of Europe as well. The principal vehicle for these has been post-colonial population movement. Global migration has increased dramatically since the middle of the twentieth century. The most striking part of this has been the level of movement to Europe, whereas previously the trend was one of movement from Europe to the 'settler colonies' of North America, southern Africa and Australasia. Initially at least, the pattern of this immigration to Europe could be closely correlated to colonial relationships. The European destination of choice for migrants from the colonies and ex-colonies tended to be their respective imperial 'motherlands'. There were a number of reasons for this and not least among them was language. Beyond this, for the skilled migrant, European recognition of educational and professional qualifications (which may originally have been exported from the imperial country) was also important. So too were the different patterns of imperial shipping and airline routes which were usually maintained after decolonization. Then, once a particular migrant community was established in the imperial country, it became a natural destination for new arrivals from the same colonies and former colonies. Often the metropolitan state would actively recruit workers from their colonies to meet labour shortages at home, particularly in the public services. It is a cliché, but undeniably true, that Britain's National Health Service and public transport systems were dependent on migrant workers in the 1950s and 1960s. In a quite literal sense, labour from the Caribbean and south Asia kept the country moving in these decades.

The same patterns of migration developed in other parts of post-imperial Europe. France was the destination of choice not just for returning *pieds noirs* after the independence of Algeria in the early 1960s. Many North Africans from Algeria – and from Tunisia and Morocco – moved to France for both economic and political reasons. They were joined by a later wave of migration from former French West Africa. By the 1980s the term *assimilation* no longer described an imperial ideal in France but a major domestic social problem. The catastrophic civil wars and social disintegration that followed Portugal's hurried departure from Africa in the mid-1970s created a major migratory movement. Hundreds of thousands of Angolan and Mozambican Africans joined the fleeing white settlers in the 'return' to what they had been taught to think of as the spiritual core of an indivisible Lusitanian entity.

A fascinating sidelight shone on this human movement in the Berlin Olympic Stadium during the final of the 2006 football World Cup. The match was played between France, one of the most 'imperial' of the former imperial powers, and Italy, a country that despite its best efforts during the twentieth century could not turn itself into a major colonial power. The Italian national team was almost wholly European in ethnicity and race, a reflection of the light footprint left by Italy's limited colonial past. In contrast, France, a colonial power of much greater range and duration, fielded a line-up dominated by black and brown faces. Captained by the incomparable Zinédine Zidane, son of Algerian immigrants to Marseilles, the team exemplified the special social composition of France which developed in the aftermath of its colonialism. And, of course, the very existence of the championship itself was a cultural manifestation of colonization: football, a sport of colonization, had become a truly global obsession. More tellingly perhaps, cricket, the sport of the English governing class, has never managed to cross the Scottish border. Yet it has long been a passion throughout the West Indies and south Asia, shipped there in the luggage of colonial administrators and educators.

Another impression of the depth of impact of colonialism in Europe is available on any evening on the high street of the smallest British town. By the 1970s south Asian and Cantonese food dominated the eating-out habits of the entire population. The availability of this post-colonial cuisine revolutionized British attitudes to food after the Second World War. Counter-claims have been made for the impact of books about Mediterranean cooking in the 1950s, but these influenced only a section of the middle class. In contrast, the local curry house had a truly democratic reach. The indigenous cuisine of France may have presented a greater obstacle to this particular colonial infil-tration, but still the streets of Paris are redolent of the flavours of North Africa and south-east Asia. In Amsterdam and other Dutch towns, the preference is Indonesian.

These may seem trivial, even flippant, examples of the enduring impact of the colonial century on Europe. But they point to a fundamental alteration in the texture of west European life. The dependence of the European economies and public services on colonial labour may have lessened by the beginning of the twenty-first century. New migrant flows, many of them from inside Europe itself, may have supplanted much of this workforce. The existence of colonial diasporas in the old imperial states has, however, transformed almost all aspects of daily life, from the character of social policy right down to national gene-pools as inter-marriage in various permutations becomes commonplace.

A final reckoning?

In the 1990s the French historian Marc Ferro concluded that in drawing up

a final balance sheet for the French, Dutch or British presence, one cannot find a single orange that was not defiled, a single apple that was not rotten. Thus ... the European historical memory has retained for itself one last privilege: that of painting its own misdeeds in dark colours and evaluating them on its own terms.

(Marc Ferro, Colonization: A Global History [1994], p. vii)

As Ferro suggests, by the last decade of the twentieth century there were few European intellectuals, beyond the small group of right-wing 'usual suspects', who would say anything in defence of colonialism. It may be that attitudes shifted slightly at the beginning of the new century. The horrors of Rwanda, Somalia, the Congo and Liberia were lurid markers of the failure of the 'African renaissance' predicted after the collapse of Apartheid South Africa. Casting the blame for these human disasters exclusively on their colonial pasts was now no longer quite as convincing as it once had been. Perhaps, some argued, the obvious dark side of colonialism should not be allowed to obscure completely the order and stability that foreign rule had brought to benighted lives. But this shift from the prevailing fin de siècle anti-colonialism did not go deep. Europe's capacity to generate its own horrors, whether in the Balkans or the former Soviet Union, was a warning against any revival of imperial complacency. Then, the western invasions of Afghanistan and Iraq re-focused attention on an essential truth: the damage caused by foreign occupation is cast widely; it afflicts all sides in the 'imperial' relationship, across all ethnic divides.

> *Perhaps an evaluation of colonialism is better approached obliquely, rather than by assembling lists of pros and cons.*

Perhaps an evaluation of colonialism is better approached obliquely, rather than by assembling lists of pros and cons. A more important question than whether colonialism was a 'good' or a 'bad' thing may be whether it was an 'avoidable' thing. In other words, is it conceivable to construct an alternative contemporary world in which colonialism never existed? By the mid-nineteenth century a yawning technology gap had opened between Europe and the global South. This had a number of effects that simply made the intensification of colonialism inevitable. First, a major part of Europe's industrial superiority lay in transport and communications. Rapid world-wide travel was now a possibility thanks to steam navigation. Other innovations, particularly in small arms, permitted ever-deeper penetration into distant tropical interiors. Unavoidably, this led to an intensification of contacts between Europe and the South.

The motives underlying these contacts were genuinely varied: the drive to trade, religious evangelism, the search for raw materials, migration and settlement. All had a role. Yet, none, despite the claims of various mono-causal theorists, was dominant to the exclusion of all others. An obviously unbalanced relationship of power – whether technological, military or economic – will eventually be mirrored in a political relationship as well. Given nineteenth-century Europe's high conceit of itself, not only in the technological realm but across the spectrum of 'progress', the expression of that unequal power through acquisitive colonialism becomes inevitable.

There is nothing inherently nineteenth century or European in this, of course. It just happened that Europe found itself in a position of relative power at a particular time. Colonialism already had a long European pedigree. But it was not a uniquely European form of behaviour. Africa, Asia and the Americas had long histories of colonial expansionism before a European foot had been set down in them. Arabs had arrived overland and by sea in west and east Africa centuries before the European 'scramble'. These newcomers exploited their relative technological superiority in unequal political relationships just as Europeans would in the future. Even within sub-Saharan Africa itself, colonialism was already widespread. By many accounts the earliest origins of the conflict between Hutus and Tutsis in Rwanda lie in the subjection of the Bantu Hutus to the power of the Tutsis who arrived from the north-east in the fifteenth century. The power of the Incas in South America was extended through the colonization of adjacent lands long before the arrival of the Spanish conquistadors. Racial attitudes were perhaps particularly marked among nineteenth-century European colonialists, but they were hardly new. They had been central to Chinese, Persian, Greek and Roman imperialism millennia earlier.

The only really significant differences setting apart the colonialism of the nineteenth and twentieth centuries from what had gone before were, first, the size of the technology gap and, secondly, the cultural milieu in which colonization took place. The first of these more or less guaranteed the success of the colonial project. Italy's humiliation in 1896 at the hands of an Abyssinian army was a unique exception to the rule of easy military victory. The facility with which colonial conquest could be achieved was taken as a kind of confirmation of its historical 'rightness'. This provides a link with the second unique aspect of the new imperialism. The intellectual climate in late nineteenth-century Europe was one in which philosophical (usually religious) justifications for the colonial project were easily culti-vated. It was not difficult in these circumstances for Europeans to convince themselves of their 'civilizing mission'.

Paradoxically, that conviction of European superiority carried the embryo of its own nemesis. European forms of political thought and organization were imposed on the colonies as part of the civilizing mission. This nourished essentially 'European' forms of territorial nationalism among the subject peoples, who took their cue from the political cultures of their colonial masters. By the middle of the twentieth century 'Westphalian' statehood had become the crowning ambition of colonial nation-alism just as it had been for the European nationalism of Czechs, Hungarians and Serbs a century earlier. 'Progressive' thought in Europe itself was meanwhile evolving and, almost without a dis-cernible change of pace, abandoning the assumption that imperialism was a permanent state.

The process by which these deep cultural shifts worked through to the policy plane was neither smooth nor uncontested, but work through they did. The Second World War – in both its political and military aspects – was critical here. The rhetoric of democracy employed by the European colonial powers, along with the exposure of their physical vulnerability, left them with no viable alternative to imperial withdrawal. There was, however, one act of colonization still left to be performed, even as the flags were changed. The independence won by the ex-colonial countries was to be exercised within structures and according to rules set down by the imperial world. There would be no escape from territorial statehood and participation in a western constructed international system.

This is where the debate about the merits and demerits of colonialism becomes in a sense irrelevant. There is a broad consensus at the beginning of the twenty-first century in both the former colonial world and in Europe that colonialism had at its heart greed, prejudice, complacency and hypocrisy rather than generosity and altruism. But it is virtually impossible to conceive of a world in which the colonial age had not existed. If we suppose that Europe had exercised a superhuman, collective self-restraint and resisted the siren calls of territorial acquisition in the tropics, what would the contemporary world look like? Would it be a more secure and prosperous place? Would the vast spaces of the global South somehow have found their own way into the system of states, the system on which such limited stability as the planet enjoys is built? While relative underdevelopment might indeed be a consequence of colonialism and a requirement of neocolonialism, would those parts of Africa and Asia wholly untouched by industrial capitalism when the colonialists arrived somehow have become strong and successful partners in the world economy? The emphasis throughout this book has been on the crucial role of colonialism in the construction of the contemporary world. Ultimately, this was a role determined by a conjunction of historical forces, and while we can challenge its morality we are left with its inevitability.

Recommended reading

Martin Holland's *The European Union and the Third World* (London: Palgrave, 2002) explores the many dimensions of Europe's relationships with its former colonies and the broader global South. W. David McIntyre provides a comprehensive introduction to the role of the Commonwealth in *A Guide to the Contemporary Commonwealth* (London: Palgrave, 2001).

The concept of cosmopolitanism is critically examined by the West African-born, British-educated and American-based writer Kwame Anthony Appiah in *Cosmopolitanism: Ethics in a World of Strangers* (London: Penguin, 2006). The accusation that cosmopolitanism approaches too closely to neocolonialism is one of the issues discussed by the contributors to the collection edited by Daniele Archibugi, *Debating Cosmopolitanism* (London: Verso, 2003).

The complex and highly contested processes of globalization are introduced in Jan Aart Scholte's accessible, but thoughtful, *Globalization: a Critical Introduction* (London: Palgrave, 2000). A.G. Hopkins' edited collection, *Globalization in World History* (London: Vintage, 2002), offers a range of perspectives on the origins of the process.

A comprehensive introduction to the concepts, historiographic and literary, of post-colonialism is provided by Robert J.C. Young's *Postcolonialism: an Historical Introduction* (Oxford: Blackwell, 2001) and Henry Schwartz and Ray Sangeeta's edited collection, *A Companion to Postcolonial Studies* (Oxford: Blackwell, 2005). Edward Said's *Orientalism: Western Conceptions of the Orient* (London: Penguin, 2003), first published in 1978, along with his *Culture and Imperialism* (London: Vintage, 1994) are seminal contributions to the discourse. David Cannadine's *Ornamentalism: How the British Saw their Empire* (London: Penguin, 2001) is, as the title suggests, a riposte to Said's view of race as the defining feature of imperialism. Cannadine argues instead that, for the British Empire at least, class was the driving dynamic.

Index